W9-BTN-491

VERMONT COLLEGE
MONTPELIER, VT.

WITHDRAWN

Every man a Phoenix

WITHDRAWN

By the same author

GEORGE HERBERT

EVERY MAN A PHOENIX

❀ ❀ ❀ ❀ ❀ ❀ ❀ ❀ ❀ ❀ ❀ ❀ ❀ ❀ ❀

Studies in
seventeenth-century
autobiography by

M A R G A R E T   B O T T R A L L

WITHDRAWN

J O H N   M U R R A Y
50 Albemarle Street
LONDON

© Margaret Bottrall 1958
Made and printed in Great Britain by
William Clowes and Sons Ltd
London and Beccles

920
B75le

Contents

18917

Acknowledgements

I am indebted to the following publishers for permission to quote from their copyright works: George Allen & Unwin Ltd, for *Richard Baxter & Margaret Charlton*, ed. J. T. Wilkinson, 1928; Cambridge University Press, for Donne's *Devotions upon Emergent Occasions*, ed. John Sparrow, 1923, and for Browne's *Religio Medici*, ed. J. J. Denonain, 1955; Clarendon Press, for Donne's *Poetical Works*, ed. H. J. C. Grierson, 1912, and for *English Literature in the Earlier Seventeenth Century*, Douglas Bush, 1945; William Collins & Sons, Ltd, for *The King's Peace*, C. V. Wedgwood, 1957; J. M. Dent & Sons, for Everyman Edition of Bunyan's *Grace Abounding*, ed. G. B. Harrison, 1928, for Everyman Edition of Baxter's *Autobiography*, ed. J. M. Lloyd Thomas, 1925, and for Cardano's *Book of My Life*, translated by Jean Stoner, 1931; Routledge & Kegan Paul Ltd for Misch's *History of Autobiography in Antiquity*, translated by E. W. Dickes, 1950; Sheed & Ward Ltd, for *The Confessions of St Augustine*, translated by F. J. Sheed, 1943; and Cresset Press, for John Aubrey's *Brief Lives*, ed. A. Powell, 1949.

I should like to thank Professor T. H. Vance, of Dartmouth College, New Hampshire, for sending me a microfilm of J. C. Major's *The Role of Personal Memoirs in English Biography*. I am also grateful to him for his interest and helpful suggestions when this book was in an embryonic stage. I owe thanks to Helen Monfries and to my son Anthony for sustained encouragement while it was being written.

M.B.

I

Introduction

Autobiography as a literary form was established in England during the seventeenth century—at first glance, a surprisingly short time ago. We are nowadays so thoroughly accustomed to the phenomenon of celebrities hastening to record their own annals in print that we find it hard to believe that three hundred and fifty years ago very few Englishmen would have dreamt of such an undertaking. Even biography was an undeveloped art during the reign of the first Elizabeth. A few historiographers there were, but the chronicling of individual lives was something new, and that an ordinary private citizen should take it upon himself to narrate his own life-story was an even more remarkable innovation.

Oddly enough, the first extant autobiography in English was written by a woman, and it does not belong, as we might expect, to the period of the Renaissance but to the close of the Middle Ages. *The Book of Margery Kempe*[1] has many affinities with the confessional saints' lives that were such favourite medieval reading; but Margery, in spite of her visions and heavenly colloquies, had an observant eye and ear for mundane things, and left a most remarkable record of life and travel in the early years of the fifteenth century. Born, bred and married in King's Lynn, she made pilgrimages to Jerusalem and Rome and St James of Compostella, and as an elderly woman journeyed to Danzig. Though much of the book is given up to her 'revelations', she deals with human relationships in the

[1] Modernised by W. Butler-Bowdon, 1936.

most frank and matter-of-fact way. She is honest enough (though obviously she feels herself much misunderstood) to set down the adverse comments of her neighbours and travelling companions, who found that she tried their patience beyond endurance with her excessive piety and uncontrollable weeping and screaming fits. *The Book of Margery Kempe* combines two types of autobiography, the factual narrative and the spiritual chronicle, which would make it remarkable even if it had been composed at a much later date. Its isolation gives it an almost freakish air, though it can be conjectured that similar lives may have been written and subsequently lost.

There were a few Elizabethan recusant priests who wrote, in Latin, accounts of their adventures and misadventures; but valuable as these are historically, they are lacking in human and personal detail. It was not until the seventeenth century that the autobiography manifested itself as a vigorous growth in England. There was no counterpart here to what happened during the great creative period of the Italian Renaissance. Instead, we had a fifteenth century that was culturally inferior to the fourteenth, and then the disruption of the Reformation. At last came Sidney, with the magic words, 'Look in thy heart and write', but in spite of his disclaimers, he wrote most of his sonnets within the well-defined Petrarchan convention; and though the tone of his *Apology for Poetry* is engagingly personal, his sense of literary decorum was quite alien to self-revelation. When, however, we come to John Donne, we encounter a man in whom the autobiographical impulse was strongly developed; and by the time that Milton reached maturity, men were ready enough to write of their personal affairs.

Milton himself in the course of his pamphleteering could not refrain from discoursing at length about his origins, his upbringing, his intellectual development, his literary ambitions and his professional life. These passages were not digressions, but very pertinent replies to the abuse that had been flung at him by political adversaries; yet the willingness with which he embarks upon them suggests that both he and his readers had a taste for the autobiographical. Though he affirms rather than analyses, we learn much from these pages about his temperament as well as about his career. No previous English poet or man of letters had attempted anything comparable, and this cannot be wholly explained in terms of Milton's egocentricity or of the provocation offered to him. A change in literary taste had come about; by the middle of the seventeenth century, the climate was favourable to self-assertion, self-scrutiny, self-revelation.

There were then, and there still are, two distinct types of autobiography. By far the commoner at the present time is the memoir, the life-story based on verifiable facts. This approximates to biography in its reliance upon external circumstance. The author, for the benefit of his contemporaries, and perhaps with one eye on posterity, recalls what he can about his ancestry, his home, his childhood and education, his public career, his distinguished friends. It is a pattern that we all recognise; and, provided that the autobiographer is not merely a celebrity but an accomplished writer too, the resulting book may be entertaining and enlightening to the general reader and valuable to the student of social history.

Besides the memoir, however, which sets out to relate how the author arrived at the point where he is standing at the time of writing, there is the other kind of autobiography, based upon self-scrutiny. Here the author is trying to explain why he is the kind of person he has turned out to be; why he thinks and behaves as he does. Inasmuch as the writer is concerned with self-knowledge, he has affinities with the philosopher, the poet and the penitent. His interest is focused upon his inner life, and outward happenings may be relegated to the background. This emphasis upon spiritual development makes the introspective essay of peculiar value to all who find the psychology of their fellows a source of unending fascination.

Manners and modes change so rapidly that memoirs soon acquire a 'period' flavour; but the self-analytical kind of autobiography is less affected by the passage of time. Intuitive and emotional ways of reacting to experience do not alter much, though intellectual attitudes do. We recognise our own moods portrayed in the literature of the ancient Hebrews and Greeks, in spite of the fact that the organisation of their outward lives differed profoundly from ours. Moreover, true self-knowledge is as elusive as ever it was. We have a new psychological terminology with which to describe our findings, but the difficult thing, now as always, is to observe accurately and dispassionately. The intelligence that watches and comments is not separated from the self which is being watched. Nor is that self static; even in memory it has chameleon qualities.

The seventeenth century was an age which favoured and fostered introspection, as no previous epoch in our history had done, and the genesis of English autobiography is largely explainable in the light of this. That is why I have chosen for the first of my autobiographers Sir Thomas Browne; for though purists may object that he does not qualify for the title, so slight is his regard for objective narrative, his *Religio Medici* is a beautiful example of the inward-looking, ruminative essay in self-exploration. Bunyan's *Grace Abounding*, though also neglectful of mundane facts, is the undoubted masterpiece among the many conversion-narratives of the period, and is an astonishing result of intense absorption in personal experience. Lord Herbert of Cherbury was a pioneer in reminiscence, and Lady Halkett an exceptionally lively, and almost unknown, memoir-writer of a rather later vintage. These two exemplify the more extrovert type of autobiography. Richard Baxter was chosen for study because he so strikingly combines the self-analytical with the historical approach.

Perhaps a word of apology is needed for omitting George Fox, whose *Journal* contains so many passages of wonderful self-revelation, and whose followers both in England and America so diligently wrote their spiritual autobiographies. It is not easy to draw a firm line that will put a discursive life-review like Baxter's in a different category from a discursive journal like Fox's; but a true autobiography differs in perspective and proportion from a journal or diary. Had Fox been admitted, Pepys and Evelyn might have come in too, and the original intention of the study would have been obscured.

What principally differentiates an autobiography from a journal is the element of re-consideration. Both provide first-hand evidence of life lived, and it may happen that the less premeditated record is truer to facts than the planned review. This latter is usually written from a vantage-point that allows a wider survey and a much more deliberate choice of the episodes to be emphasised. There is consequently greater scope for self-deception, and for that slight degree of falsification which so often accompanies the ordering of material for literary effect. But it is the emergence of autobiography as a literary *genre* that is the subject of this study. If the auto-biographical impulse itself were being surveyed, diaries and journals would certainly have to be included. One would have to reckon, too, with poetry and fiction, for the impulse to crystallise the individual personal experience can be satisfied through a variety of means. Wordsworth's *Prelude* is one of the most perfect expressions of the autobiographical impulse in our literature; and how many novelists, from Dickens and Charlotte Brontë to Somerset Maugham and Evelyn Waugh, have made unashamed use of autobiographical material!

Indeed, a consideration of the autobiographical impulse would need to go outside literature and to take cognisance of the self-portraits of painters. All that I am trying to do in these few chapters is to examine some early and varied specimens of English autobiography and to suggest reasons why the climate of the seventeenth century was favourable to this form of self-expression.

II

'My selfe am Center of my circling thought . . .'

Since every man is by nature self-centred and to some extent self-assertive, we might expect that autobiography would be as primitive a form of literature as drama or epic; but it is nothing of the kind. The wish to record personal achievements for the benefit of posterity is ancient enough; there are numerous Egyptian and Assyrian inscriptions written in the first person; but they merely perpetuate names and actions, they transmit nothing of the individual qualities of those whom they commemorate. Fragments of self-portraiture may be found in epistles, commentaries, prophetic writings, lyric poems from the ancient world; yet true autobiography is a late-comer on the literary scene.

The description of an individual human life by the individual himself, who possesses a store of recollected experiences available to nobody else—this cannot be accomplished without a high degree of self-consciousness. Even the straightforward chronicle of an active life involves the constant exercise of judgement and the endeavour to be an impartial critic of one's own past. From the superabundance of memories, the truly relevant facts must be selected and arranged in a coherent and significant pattern. Far more complex in origin and scope than the factual memoirs are the autobiographies in which men seek to chart their spiritual histories. The writing of these demands exceptional self-knowledge and integrity. Genuine autobiography can only be written by someone acutely aware of his own existence as an individual, someone able to reflect on the nature of his actions within the framework of his total experience.

Memoirs may be prompted by the desire—particularly active in times of rapid social change—to leave to friends or descendants authentic historical testimony; or by the wish to increase and assure an already achieved reputation. The motives behind introspective autobiographies are less easily discernible. The recording of spiritual growth requires a finer discrimination and a far more sensitive awareness of the soul's uniqueness than the narration of verifiable events. Benvenuto Cellini's autobiography is a masterpiece among chronicles of achievement, but its range is comparatively limited. Frank, minutely detailed, exuberant, it is a fascinating self-portrait and it gives us a vivid insight into the life of *cinquecento* Italy; but it is conceived in an extrovert temper, and does not attempt any exploration of the inner man. The writer who does embark on such a voyage of discovery may be impelled by either religious or humanist motives; but whether, like St Augustine or John Bunyan, he sets out to trace the workings of grace in his soul, or whether, like Montaigne or Sir Thomas Browne, he tries to account for his own idiosyncrasies, he is keenly aware that the enterprise is a difficult one and that vain-glory will not get him very far.

Some degree of self-assertion must, however, be present even in the most apparently humble and tentative auto-biographer. Utter humility would annihilate the autobiographical impulse. Anyone who genuinely felt that he was 'a worm and no man' would be wholly unable to write about his own concerns or to conceive that other people could be interested in knowing anything about him. Sustained by the inner conviction that he is a being of some consequence, a good autobiographer must be simultaneously self-centred and detached; humble enough to be on his guard against attitudinising, able to keep his attention untiringly on the object of his scrutiny, and persuaded of the ultimate value of what he is doing.

The wish to assert the value of one's own individuality is not always displayed so unaffectedly as in the boastful pages of Lord Herbert of Cherbury; it may be disguised as penitential self-detestation; but it cannot be eliminated. If it is reinforced by the wish to discover how the writer's individuality comes to be the unique thing that it is, the autobiography becomes more than a chronicle, more than a case-history; it becomes— as in the hands of Proust, though he complicates it with fictitious invention—a potent instrument for extending our knowledge of human nature.

The kind of truth to be looked for in an autobiography is not, and cannot be, the factual truth of a historical chronicle. External facts may, indeed, be faithfully registered; but as Georg Misch wisely points out in the introductory chapter of *A History of Autobiography in Antiquity*, '. . . in the reproduction of inward, and especially of religious experiences, autobiography is a field of self-delusion. How, indeed, can it possibly bear witness to anything more than the extent of the self-knowledge of the individual at the time when, looking back on the past, he attempts to survey and assess his life as a whole (p. 12)?' Nevertheless, in so far as it is the creative expression of the writer's mind, it cannot be otherwise than true, with the same kind of truthfulness as poetry possesses. The author mirrors himself, almost involuntarily, in the very way that he considers his life as an entity and discriminates between significant and unimportant elements in it. Though his handling of facts may be provably inaccurate or tendentious, his total picture has an authenticity that is beyond dispute.

'Truth, naked unblushing Truth, the first virtue of serious history, must be the sole recommendation of this personal narrative.' Thus Gibbon speaks of his *Autobiography*; and though we cannot fail to observe that he actually took great care to drape Truth in conventional and becoming garments, it may be admitted that his evasions and complacencies do convey, beneath the public face of the distinguished historian, the handicapped, sensitive, easily affronted man whose existence is never examined, but only betrayed by occasional turns of phrase. Mere veracity, in any case, is not enough to create a fine autobiography. There is little of interest in the candid records of dull or trivial minds. Yet without a genuine regard for truth no writer can achieve a self-portrait that is a convincing human likeness. The great autobiographers are those best able to understand and honour the subtler demands of truth; those whose personal integrity is matched by their artistic and critical discrimination.

A painter intent on a self-portrait studies himself in a mirror; what he looks like now, at this moment, is his concern. He may, as he paints, reflect upon the experiences that have gone to give him his actual appearance, but this is not essential to his task of conveying a likeness of his present self. The autobiographer has no fixed image of himself to contemplate; what he is now cannot be understood without a consideration of his own past. It is the development of his own identity that he must scrutinise. He is called upon to be philosopher as well as historian.

Moreover, even the most intelligently introspective writer can only produce true autobiography when the prevailing philosophical climate favours the study of personality. Marcus Aurelius, for example, lived at an unpropitious time. When there exists a well-defined social hierarchy, and certain ideals of moral virtue are accepted by all thinking men, the idiosyncratic is of small account. The autobiographical impulse is favoured by disturbed social conditions. When traditional structures are breaking down, when men are no longer conscious of a clear pattern by which to order their moral existence, when the sense of belonging to a community is lost, then the value of individual personality has the chance to be keenly apprehended and asserted. The conditions of his world favoured the composition of St Augustine's *Confessions*; but the view of Man prevalent throughout Christendom during the Middle Ages did not foster the autobiographical impulse much more than the accepted assumptions of Greece and Rome had done so. Dante, by framing the poems of *La Vita Nuova* in the narrative of a personal adventure, was some generations ahead of his time, even though in Italy the cult of the individual was established much earlier than elsewhere.

It is not easy to account for the fact that the *Confessions* of St Augustine remained for about a thousand years without a true successor; for though two strains in the *Confessions*—the penitential and the devotional—are echoed in many of the medieval lives of saints, there is no trace in these of the ransacking of the inward life of the spirit which makes Augustine's book so vital and so timeless.

When an Augustinian friar in Paris gave a pocket-sized copy of the *Confessions* to Petrarch, he may well have hoped that it would move him to amendment of life. In a sense it did so, but only because Petrarch seized upon the self-analytical, autobiographical elements in the book, which so fascinated him that he seemed to be reading the story of his own inner life. The little volume went with him everywhere, even on his celebrated mountain climb, and in 1342 he wrote three dialogues between himself and St Augustine in which he carried out a searching analysis of his own character. These Latin dialogues, which Petrarch called *Secretum Meum*, were not published until after his death.[1] Though their cultivated, secular tone is very different from Augustine's, they do mirror the conflicts of a divided spirit. By stern questions and admonitions the conscience (under the guise of Augustine) forces into the open many weaknesses which self-deception had disguised; slackness of will is the major fault, but distraction of mind, irrational melancholy and an insatiable thirst for fame are all laid bare. The book is much less rich in autobiographical detail than many of Petrarch's letters, but as a new venture into introspective writing it is of great interest and importance. That Petrarch, who did so much to initiate the age of humanism, should be the rediscoverer of Augustine the autobiographer suggests that only in a time of cultural unrest could this aspect of the saint's genius be fully appreciated. The age of faith, so strongly institutionalised, with its rigid systems of rewards and penalties, encouraged the human soul to seek salvation rather than self-knowledge. Even Petrarch's dialogues have a framework that suggests the relationship between a stern father-confessor and a rather reluctant penitent. Nevertheless, the interest in the actual vagaries of the human spirit is very evident, and in the third dialogue, that deals with love and fame, the balance between the two elements in the divided soul is kept so evenly that the final effect is not one of contrition.

Although Protestant England in the sixteenth century abjured the confessional, the seeking of spiritual guidance in times of necessity was always provided for in the Prayer Book, and even among dissenters of the seventeenth century it was commonly resorted to. It would therefore be misleading, though it is tempting, to suggest a causal connection between the disappearance of the practice of auricular confession and the

[1] Translated by W. H. Draper as *Petrarch's Secret, or The Soul's Conflict with Passion*, 1911.

appearance of self-examining autobiographies. The Puritan habit of sharing religious experiences through public testifying certainly encouraged one type of autobiography that was common in the seventeenth century, the conversion narrative; but the problem of self-knowledge was approached from a number of other angles besides the religious. Since the Renaissance, in every country there have been men of speculative, scientific or sceptical turns of mind, who discovered that one sure method of learning more about mankind in general was to study the man nearest to hand—the self, unique yet representative.

The Elizabethan age, notwithstanding its persistent concern with religious and moral issues, was active rather than contemplative in temper. During the reign of Elizabeth, the boundaries of the physical world were amazingly enlarged, and the little world of man was explored with equal energy and daring in the theatre. The dramatic method of exploring human nature, however, is diametrically opposed to the introspective and autobiographical. Although the dramatist, like any other poet, depends upon the resources of his own experience for the creation of character and action, he cannot afford to intrude himself and his personal concerns upon the spectator. If he makes himself strongly felt, whether by tendentious speeches or by imperfectly disguised sympathies, the organic life of the play is imperilled. Of course it is his moral judgements that give each drama its peculiar colour, and not all playwrights have avoided the didactic pitfalls as subtly as Shakespeare; but ideally the dramatist becomes anonymous, a powerful and transparent lens. No poet has told us more than Shakespeare about the unpredictable strangeness of human nature or the potentialities for good and evil in the spirit of man; but in his complete absorption in his themes he eliminates himself.

Elizabethan and Jacobean drama enlarged the ordinary man's conception of humanity by presenting characters in relation to historical and political circumstances, as in the chronicle and Roman plays; or, in comedy, by holding up to ridicule the social follies of the age or by setting mortals in fairy-tale environments; but pre-eminently in tragedy, when man is seen in stark relation to his destiny. As long as the Elizabethan theatre flourished, the problems and contradictions of the human condition could be presented in terms of action, rather than as subjects for meditation; but by the end of Shakespeare's life, the patronage of the drama had passed into a sophisticated Court circle, and the public that counted most was one that preferred spectacle to rhetoric and melodrama to tragedy. Serious criticism of human nature therefore had to find expression in non-dramatic forms.

The need for a systematic study of Man had already been felt and expressed. It is not surprising to find Bacon, with his passion for scientific knowledge, deploring in *The Advancement of Learning* (1605) the philosophers' insistence on abstract ethics and their neglect of psychology and political science. In *De Augmentia Scientiarum* he specified his requirements for a Science of Man, to consist of investigation into the workings of the human mind and body and a study of the behaviour of man in society. In his *Essays* he commended Machiavelli for writing about what men actually do, instead of moralising about what they ought to do; and it has been suggested that the practical slant of the *Essays* is at least partly due to Bacon's wish to contribute 'to that realistic knowledge of the genus *homo* without which the individual cannot prescribe for his own needs nor the statesman for the needs of society.'[1] In Bacon's lifetime great advances were made in anatomical and

---

[1] Douglas Bush, *English Literature in the earlier Seventeenth Century*, Oxford University Press, 1945, p. 185.

physiological knowledge, thanks to the experiments of such men as Fabricius, van Helmont and Harvey; but he was far ahead of his time in his conception of the need for systematic study of individual and social psychology.

A much less massive figure than Bacon, yet because of his non-scientific interests an almost more valuable witness to the temper of the age, is Sir John Davies. He was a distinguished lawyer, for much of his life Attorney-General for Ireland. In 1599—the earliness of the date is remarkable—he published a poem with the significant title *Nosce Teipsum*. It is a masterly work, and the fact that it went into five editions during its author's lifetime suggests that its contemplative quatrains epitomised ideas common to many of his readers. In this poem Davies laments man's ignorance of his own nature, and sets out to remedy one aspect of the deficiency by a closely argued metaphysical examination of the nature of the soul. There is a certain pathos in the discrepancy between the bravery of his intention and the actual psychological knowledge at his disposal. Even physiological studies had not advanced very far by the end of the sixteenth century, and in psychology the masters were still Plato, Aristotle and the schoolmen. Progress in anatomical knowledge had, however, prompted intelligent men to ask new and urgent questions about the relation of the soul to the body. Dissection provoked the question, where does the soul reside? To what organ can it be related? *What is it?*

Davies works out an answer along traditional lines, Christian modified by Neoplatonic thought. It is not the argument of the poem, excellently sustained though it is, that breaks new ground, but his brilliant exposition, in the introductory stanzas, of the intellectual climate of his times.

Davies compares the enterprise of the navigators in

exploring the physical world with the indifference shown by philosophers to the investigation of Man himself:

> We that acquaint our selves with every *Zone*,
>   And passe both *Tropiks*, and behold the *Poles*,
> When we come home, are to our selves unknowne,
>   And unacquainted still with our owne *Soules*. (st. xxv)[1]

He doubts whether a man can ever arrive at adequate self-knowledge, since he believes that Reason is an imperfect and corrupted instrument:

> What can we know? or what can we discerne?
>   When *Error* chokes the windowes of the mind;
> The diverse formes of things, how can we learne,
>   That have bene ever from our birth-day blind?
>
> When *Reason's* lampe, which (like the *Sunne* in skie)
>   Throughout Man's little world her beams did spread,
> Is now become a Sparkle, which doth lie
>   Under the Ashes, halfe extinct, and dead;
>
> How can we hope, that through the Eye and Eare,
>   This dying Sparkle, in this cloudie place,
> Can recollect these beames of knowledge cleare,
>   That were infus'd in the first minds by grace? (xv–xvii)

He is naturally sceptical about accepting the conclusions of the human mind, which is so unconscious of its own biases:

> For why should we the busie Soule beleeve,
>   When boldly she concludes of that, and this,
> When of her selfe she can no judgement geve,
>   Nor how, nor whence, nor where, nor what she is? (xxii)

Nevertheless, he has no wish to curb the eagerly enquiring spirit; rather, he suggests that it has been strangely negligent:

---

[1] *Poems* of Sir John Davies, reproduced in facsimile from the first editions in the Huntingdon Library. Edited with introduction and notes by Claire Howard, Columbia University Press, 1941.

> We seeke to know the moving of each spheare,
>   And the straunge cause of th'ebs and flouds of *Nile*;
> But of that clocke within our breasts we beare,
>   The subtill motions we forget the while.   (xxiv)

Davies is not concerned to examine his own individual nature in this poem, and only a few stanzas are obliquely autobiographical—those which deal magnificently with the theme of Affliction's power to teach; but he admits that the starting-point for his investigations into the nature of the soul is self-scrutiny:

> My selfe am Center of my circling thought,
>   Onely my selfe I studie, learne, and knowe . . .   (xlii)

Nosce Teipsum is an exceptionally lucid poem, metaphysical in the strict meaning of the word, but quite free from the metaphysical conceits which characterise Donne's *Progresse of the Soule*, and far more impersonal. It is typical of Donne that he associates man's ignorance of the soul with his ignorance of the body:

> Poore soule, in this thy flesh what dost thou know? . . .
> Thou art too narrow, wretch, to comprehend
> Even thy selfe: yea, though thou wouldst but bend
> To know thy body   (p. 258)[1]

In spite of the advances made in medicine and the natural sciences during the sixteenth century, the medieval notions of the relation of the soul to the body and of man to the cosmos persisted long. Donne begins one of his Holy Sonnets with the lines:

> I am a little world made cunningly
> Of Elements, and an Angelike spright . . .   (p. 324)

[1] Page numbers after Donne quotations refer to Grierson's edition of the *Poetical Works*, 1912.

Characteristically, however, the passage from *The Second Anniversary* cited above continues with a reminder that the new learning has made people as uncertain about the constitution of their bodies as they traditionally are about the nature of their souls:

> Have not all soules thought
> For many ages, that our body 'is wrought
> Of Ayre, and Fire, and other Elements?
> And now they thinke of new ingredients,
> And one Soule thinks one, and another way
> Another thinkes, and 'tis an even lay. (p. 259)

These few instances will serve to indicate that at the beginning of the seventeenth century there was in England, among literary men, an awareness that man's 'little world' was still largely undiscovered. The mapping process had, however, already begun in Italy and France. In 1574 Girolamo Cardano, an eminent physician of Milan, set out at the age of seventy-four to write a natural history of himself. *De Vita Propria Liber*[1] is the first autobiography conceived in a scientific spirit. This highly original book did not exert an immediate influence, for it was not published until 1643, but the early date of its composition is worth noting. Almost at the same time Montaigne began the study and delineation of himself. In 1580 appeared the first two books of the *Essais*, and in 1588 the third book, the most personal of the three.

Although the two men were temperamentally very unlike, and produced works so different in literary quality that they can scarcely be compared, they both clearly recognised that they were pioneers. Montaigne says of his *Essais*, 'C'est le seul livre au monde de son espece, d'un dessein farouche et extravagant.' (Bk II, viii) Cardano remarks:

> An account of this nature is by its own character a most difficult thing to write, and so much the more for me as I reflect

[1] Trans. by Jean Stoner as *The Book of My Life*, 1931.

that those who have been wont to read the autobiographical books of writers are not used to seeing such a straightforward narrative set down as I purpose to publish. Some have committed themselves to writing as they think they ought to be, like Antoninus; others have, indeed, given true accounts, but with all their shortcomings carefully suppressed, as did Josephus. But I prefer to do service to truth, though well aware that he who transgresses the conventions cannot offer the same excuses as suffice for other mistakes. (p. 49)

Both had made the exciting discovery that the man who studies himself has an inexhaustible mass of data at his disposal —data not available to anyone else in a comparable degree of completeness. The only living person who can be intimately known is one's self. Each man is unique, and therefore worthy of study for his own sake; at the same time, he is a member of the human race, and therefore by studying the characteristics of one specimen it is possible to learn more about the genus.

These considerations were common to Cardano and Montaigne, but the man of letters was more sensitive than the scientist to the elusiveness of a man's true self. Perceiving that the investigating mind is itself inconsistent, Montaigne was sceptical about the possibility of arriving at more than an approximation to truth in any department of knowledge not susceptible of mathematical proof. His explorations are more tentative than those of Cardano and less methodical; his conclusions have a far greater attraction for the general reader, because his intermittent interest in himself is related to his ceaseless interest in human behaviour.

The limits of Cardano's book are sharply defined and its tone is dry. He begins with the observation that his birth would not have taken place if his mother had not failed to procure an abortion; and, as might be expected of an eminent medical man, he records many details about his physical constitution. Although his life contained some sensational episodes, though he made a professional journey to Scotland, and though he met many distinguished people in the course of his career, he is not in the least concerned to entertain his readers. His object is to record all the facts about himself that seemed to him in his old age relevant to his development as an individual. This attempt to draw up a case-history from personal recollections is so modern an enterprise that one discovers with something of a shock that Cardano attached great importance to horoscopes and was in many ways superstitious and credulous; but he was scrupulously frank, and justified his claim to do service to truth. Because, however, he contented himself with accuracy, and preferred exactitude of detail to philosophical speculation or picturesque narrative, his book belongs to the annals of psychology rather than to those of literature.

Montaigne did not attempt a formal autobiography; indeed, his *Essais* tell us very little about his public life, and such facts as we are given about his youth and education are not set down more systematically than are the casual comments which he supplies about the details of his later private life. System was abhorrent to him; in Florio's phrase, he had 'a skipping wit.' It was only slowly that he conceived the project of portraying himself, for the earlier essays are not directly personal; gradually he becomes more intimate, and finally almost garrulous, no triviality being too insignificant for inclusion. In spite of the humorous, deprecating tone that he often uses, Montaigne is intensely serious about his self-portraiture. He reckons that he has the necessary aptitudes. In the first place, he has an inexhaustible interest in the subject to be delineated: 'Chacun regarde devant soy; moy, je regarde dedans moy; je n'ay affaire qu'à moy, je me considère sans cesse, je me contrerolle, je me gouste.' (II, xiii, *De L'Expérience*)[1]

[1] This and subsequent quotations in French are from the edition of the *Essais* by Tilley and Boase, 3rd Ed., 1954.

Besides this tireless self-absorption, Montaigne possesses the scrupulous regard for truth which is necessary for the attainment of his end: 'Pour la parfaire, je n'ay besoing d'y apporter que la fidélité; celle-là y est, la plus sincère et pure qui se trouve.' (III, ii, *Du Repentir*)

What redeems the apparent trivialities is Montaigne's grasp of the fact that in studying and portraying himself, he is registering the vagaries of human nature: 'Chaque homme porte la forme entière de l'humaine condition.' (Ibid.) Each individual is wayward, incalculable, ultimately mysterious; how can he hope to understand his fellows except by a sympathetic extension of such knowledge of human nature as he has reached by introspection? Pascal criticised Montaigne for being so incessantly preoccupied with his ego, but it was not a narrow or petty self-centredness.

'O my God! what a clod of moving Ignorance is Man! when all his industry cannot instruct him, what himself is; when he knows not that, whereby he knows that he does not know it . . .'[1] In these words Owen Felltham, writing in the 1620s, expressed the same sense of the intelligent man's predicament as Sir John Davies had put forward in *Nosce Teipsum*. What do we, what can we, know about ourselves? Socrates, the Stoics and the Epicureans had all urged the importance of self-knowledge, and the rediscovery of the classical moralists, especially Seneca and Plutarch, had produced a large harvest of moral disquisitions in England, as in every country affected by the Renaissance. Nevertheless, there were many difficulties confronting the seventeenth-century Englishman seeking to understand the nature of his own being. He was the heir of Christian as well as of classical culture, but he had lost an infallible Church, and he was also aware that Man's traditional place in the centre of the universe had been

1 *Resolves*, 8th imp. 1661, p. 112.

challenged by the discoveries of Copernicus. Consequently it was natural that he should be more inclined to study human nature by means of self-scrutiny than to dogmatise or generalise about it. Even if Montaigne had not shown the way, it would surely have been discovered by someone who shared his dilemma. As it was, his example gave an immense impetus to other sceptical and enquiring minds to turn their attention upon their own idiosyncrasies.

In the seventeenth century, as never before, Englishmen introduced themselves without a cloak of anonymity to their fellows. No doubt it was the instability of the times that prompted many to set down their comments on life for the benefit of their descendants or moved them to vindicate their reputations; but if there had not already been a diffused and general sense of the worth of individuality, autobiography could not have flourished as it did. Donne commented with his habitual cogent brilliance:

> For every man alone thinkes he hath got
> To be a Phoenix, and that there can bee
> None of that kind, of which he is, but hee.   (p. 238)

Many of those who committed their memoirs to paper were far from being true phoenixes. Robert Greene's *Groatsworth of Wit bought with a Million of Repentance* is a rather racy precursor of hundreds of conversion narratives, in which sinners vie with one another in echoing Greene's claim to be 'a meere Reprobate, the child of Sathan, one wipt out of the booke of life, and as an outcast from the face and favor of God.' By the time of the Restoration, when John Bunyan, that genius among 'mechanick preachers', produced his *Grace Abounding*, the protestant and the humanist currents in England had slowly worked together on the national consciousness to a point where the reasonably articulate man had become aware of his own worth as a unique person, and was ready to transmit that awareness through the written word.

Donne himself is a figure very relevant to any study of the autobiographical impulse in seventeenth-century England. No previous poet had been so concerned to stamp his own individual image on his creations. The most significant of his writings in this connection, however, are not the love-poems but the poems addressed to God and the *Devotions upon Emergent Occasions*. Here the tension between private and public intention is greatest. Donne is unburdening himself in passionate prayer, searching his conscience in a desperate illness—yet he circulates these poems and publishes these meditations. Originally he cannot have had any readers in mind when he wrote the *Devotions*,[1] for they were drafted during the winter of 1623 when he was in the grip of a fever from which he was not expected to recover. As soon, however, as he was, against all expectations, restored to health, he revised them and had them printed, so that this little book is one of the very few that appeared during its author's lifetime.

The conscious motive behind the publication of this volume was undoubtedly edification. Donne was deeply concerned with the salvation of souls, and he rightly supposed that the transcript of his own experiences might help others towards ardour of devotion and amendment of life. Yet *Devotions upon Emergent Occasions* is utterly different from the normal book of spiritual counsel. When we read *Holy Living* or *Holy Dying*, we are impressed by the wisdom and charity (as well as the eloquence) of Jeremy Taylor, but we get no vivid impression of his personality, nor is it in the least necessary that we should. Donne's *Devotions*, however, is primarily a book of penitential self-revelation. In it we are enabled to follow the wrestlings of his mind and spirit as they grappled

[1] Edited by John Sparrow (Scholar of Winchester College), 1923.

with the topics that concerned him most intimately in his extremity—sin, repentance, death, judgement, his own chances of eternal happiness.

The book is systematically arranged as a series of reflections, each springing from some episode in his illness, and each divided into three parts—a Meditation upon human conditions, an Expostulation or Debatement with God, and a Prayer, in which the arguments of the foregoing sections are resolved at a more exalted level. The extraordinary activity of Donne's mind derives a universal application from each particular occasion; the arrival of the king's physician, or the appearance of spots on his skin, are typical pretexts that fire his imagination, his reason and his devotion. When, for instance, 'They apply Pidgeons, to draw the vapors from the Head', he is moved to reflect:

> . . . wee are not onely *passive*, but *active* too, to our own destruction. But what have I done, either to *breed*, or to *breath* these vapors? They tell me it is my *Melancholy*; Did I infuse, did I drinke in *Melancholy* into my selfe? It is my *thoughtfulnesse*; was I not made to thinke? It is my *study*; doth not my *Calling* call for that? I have don nothing, wilfully, perversely, toward it, yet must suffer in it, die by it. . . . I doe nothing upon my selfe, and yet am mine own *Executioner*. (*Devotions*, p. 69)

Not the common plight of man reduced to depression through illness, but the precise plight of John Donne, that is what he presents; even more forcefully in a passage that a less intrepid divine might have feared to include:

> I have this weak and childish frowardness too, I cannot sit up, and yet am loth to go to bed; shall I find thee in bed? oh, have I alwaies done so? The bed is not ordinarily thy Scene, thy Climate: Lord, dost thou not accuse me, dost thou not reproach to mee, my former sinns, when thou layest mee upon this bed? (p. 12)

It would give a false impression of the book to insist exclusively on the autobiographical element in it. These communings of Donne's soul with God have the same religious exaltation, the same passionate sincerity, as his hymns and holy sonnets show. As a priest, he cared intensely about the eternal welfare of his own and of other human souls, and the *Devotions* record his wrestlings in penitential prayer. Yet it cannot be denied that self-display was as powerful a motive with Donne as self-scrutiny. His macabre determination to dress up in his shroud and pose for his own funeral effigy illustrates the complexity of his attitude. In a sense, he was humiliating himself by exhibiting his poor wasted mortal frame; at the same time, he was out to impress. Up to the last moment of his life, he wanted to make the image and likeness of John Donne memorable, striking, unique.

His consuming interest in the validity of his own experience links him with Sir Thomas Browne. The assurance with which he makes this experience available and applicable to other men springs from the conviction which both he and Browne shared with Montaigne—the certainty that every individual is inextricably involved in mankind. 'Chaque homme porte la forme entière de l'humaine condition,' or, as Donne put it, 'No man is an Island, intire of itself.' Donne, of course, had theological reasons to account for his sense of being 'involved in Mankinde'. The argument that God is the Father of all could justify his conviction that what happened to him, John Donne, had repercussions far beyond the merely personal and private. He was prepared to anatomise himself, to expose himself to others, secure in the certainty that man is not cut off from his fellows in isolation but is linked to them by the very pains and passions that he, as an individual, experiences.

If Donne in his tireless and eloquent introspection is a forerunner of Sir Thomas Browne, so too are the essayists who avowedly took their cue from Montaigne and introduced the autobiographical note into a form of writing that in Bacon's hands had remained aphoristic and impersonal. Even when Bacon enlarged and polished his original collection of ten brief pieces, he did not explore the discursive possibilities of the essay. This was left to Sir William Cornwallis, whose first volume was published in 1600 when its author was only twenty-one.[1]

These essays vary a good deal in length and scope and not all betray the influence of Montaigne, though he particularly praises 'that Noble French Knight' for his easy, well-bred handling of moral issues and learned topics. Some are lengthy disquisitions, strongly Senecan in tone, and stiffened by the references to Greek and Roman moralists which any Elizabethan with pretensions to culture was bound to employ. Others are rather tedious examinations of specific virtues and their contrary vices. But there are a number in which Cornwallis's natural propensity for chatting about his own concerns is very pleasantly exhibited. The trifle entitled *Of Alehouses* begins: 'I write this in an Alehouse, into which I am driven by night, which would not give me leave to finde out an honester harbour. I am without any company but Inke and Paper, and them I use in stead of talking to my selfe.' (p. 67) It was, of course, from Montaigne that he had caught this informal, self-revealing accent; but there is in Cornwallis a confidingness that makes him interesting to students of English autobiography.

Owen Felltham, whose *Resolves* were published in 1620 and frequently reprinted, was a much more accomplished and attractive writer than Cornwallis; but in spite of consistently using the first person singular in his essays, he preserved a far greater degree of reticence. His ostensible purpose was to examine some moral or general topic in order to arrive at a

[1] *Essayes*, ed. D. C. Allen, Baltimore, 1946.

conclusion or resolution embodying his own attitude. It is only obliquely, through his recorded opinions, that we get a picture of a charming and magnanimous young man, sober in judgement but quick in fancy. Owen Felltham states his opinions with a modest assurance that is engaging, but he very rarely recounts an actual incident in which he has taken part, and when he does so it is with an air of apology. The autobiographical impulse was less strong in him than in Cornwallis; yet there is enough personal confession in the *Resolves* to make him a precursor of Sir Thomas Browne.

Felltham's deeply-felt Christianity pervades his writings, though it is variegated by an occasional Platonic touch, as when he says: 'When I see the most enchanting beauties that Earth can show me, there is something far more glorious; methinks I see a kind of higher perfection, peeping through the frailty of a face. . . .'[1] Or, speaking of the soul: 'The Conscience, the Character of God stampt in it, and the apprehension of Eternity, do all prove it a shoot of Everlastingnesse.' (p. 112) But it is when he analyses his feelings about the Puritans, or examines the possibility of choice in religions, that he closely resembles the serene Anglican piety of Browne:

> Assuredly, though Faith be above Reason, yet there is a reason to be given of our Faith. He is a Fool that believes he knows neither what nor why. Among all the Diversities of Religion that the world holds, I think we may stand with most safety, to take that, which makes most for God's glory and Man's quiet. I confess, in all the Treatises of Religion that ever I saw, I find none that I should so soon follow, as that of the Church of England. (p. 30)

This appeared in print more than twenty years before the famous passage in *Religio Medici*:

> . . . there is no Church whose every part so squares unto my conscience, whose articles, constitutions, and customes seem so

1 *Resolves*, 1661 edition, p. 24.

consonant unto reason, and as it were framed to my particular devotion, as this whereof I hold my beliefe, the Church of England.[1]

Though Felltham was young when he published his *Resolves*, they do not betray the faults of immaturity, and if his reflections are sometimes commonplace, his style is never dull and sometimes it dances with vitality. He occupies a place somewhere between the guarded Bacon and the erratic Cornwallis; but to Cornwallis must be given the credit of the greater innovation, in that he imitated for the first time in England —even before Florio's translation had appeared—the personal, autobiographical manner originated by Montaigne.

It is not my purpose to try to establish definite links between these earlier adventurers into the fields of introspection and our first genuine essayist in autobiography, Sir Thomas Browne. Rather I want to suggest that there was in England, during the first twenty years of the seventeenth century, an interest in individual psychology more meditative and enquiring than ever before, and that this was favourable to the establishment of autobiography as a *genre*.

The popularity of character-sketches, on the Theophrastan model, was at its height in Jacobean times; and when people begin to enjoy discussing psychological types, they are in the right frame of mind for reading or writing autobiographies. Joseph Hall's *Characters of Virtues and Vices* came out as early as 1608, and Overbury's essays appeared between 1614 and 1621. When Ben Jonson printed a revised version of *Every Man Out of His Humour*, in 1616, he added a series of brief, satirical pen-portraits, 'The Characters of the Persons'. Among them is a picture of himself, under the guise of Asper: 'He is of an ingenious and free spirit, eager, and constant in reproof,

[1] *Religio Medici*, ed. J. J. Denonain, Cambridge University Press, 1955, p. 8.

without fear controlling the world's abuses. One, whom no servile hope of gain, or frosty apprehension of danger, can make to be a parasite, either to time, place or opinion.'[1] Later in the century, the historians took over the 'Character', and produced an incomparable array of true-to-life portraits. It is the distinctive contribution of this age to the art of biography. The art of autobiography has a less obvious connection with the literary pen-portrait of the Theophrastan type, yet the link is there. It is the common taste for character-analysis. As has already been noted, autobiography is only likely to thrive when the study of individual personality is assumed to be natural and valuable. This assumption no intelligent man of the seventeenth century would have disputed.

[1] *Ben Jonson.* The Mermaid Series, Vol. I, p. 113.

III

Browne's 'Religio Medici'

In the rough autobiographical notes left by the antiquary John Aubrey, there is an entry referring to an incident that had impressed itself upon him more than fifty years earlier: '1642, *Religio Medici* published, which first opened my understanding, which I carried to Easton, with Sir Kenelm Digby.'[1]

What was it about this book that so struck the seventeen-year-old boy? He had just gone up to Oxford—'my beloved Oxon', he calls it—and his 'inventive and philosophical head' was beginning to delight in the books and music and congenial company that the university offered to a country-bred young scholar. Already Aubrey was an investigator; he had been one ever since, as a little boy, he had watched the carpenters and masons on his father's estate, and had wished himself lucky enough to live in a city like Bristol, where he could have watched clock-makers and locksmiths as well. It was not only the construction of things that fascinated him; he had wanted even as a child to learn all that he could about the past. At seventeen, then, his own inclinations were sufficiently set for him to recognise a kindred spirit in the author of *Religio Medici*. When he says that the book first opened his understanding he may be referring to its metaphysical and religious content; but he is more likely to mean that it revealed to him the endless possibilities inherent in the study of a human personality. Aubrey's own energies were to be engaged rather in the study of other men's lives than in the exploration of

[1] *Brief Lives*, ed. A. Powell, 1939, p. 16.

himself; but he could see something excitingly new in the informal, discursive way in which this anonymous doctor wrote about his beliefs, and in the unflagging attention which he gave to his own idiosyncrasies. He may have recognised that Browne's intellectual curiosity was of the same type as his own—inexhaustible, but not strenuous.

The second part of Aubrey's note indicates that he took *Religio Medici* home with him, together with the *Observations* which Sir Kenelm Digby had written at top speed after he had sat up most of the night reading the book in a pirated edition, on the enthusiastic recommendation of Edward Sackville, fourth Earl of Dorset.[1] Digby, 'the wonder of his age', 'learning's best advancer', 'the ornament of England', was at this time imprisoned in Winchester House. As one of the most prominent Roman Catholics in the country, and a devoted adherent of Henrietta Maria, the Parliamentarians did not care to have him at large, raising money and troops for the Royalist cause. He was already a well-known virtuoso, as well equipped as any man in England to challenge Browne on scientific issues; and his interest in theology and metaphysics was intense. For a period of five years, perhaps for motives of political expediency, Digby had forsaken his native Romanism for the Church of England; but by 1642 this secession was well behind him, and he was not disposed to approve of the easy-going Anglicanism of this anonymous physician. His commentary is often captious, sometimes careless—scarcely surprising, if he did indeed dash it off in a day, as he claimed. He excuses himself to Dorset for 'daring to consider any moles in that face, which you had marked for a

[1] Actually, these *Observations* were not printed till 1643, when they were the occasion for the publication of the first authorised edition of *Religio Medici*, with the writer's name and explanatory preface; but Aubrey, like Digby himself, might have read the pirated 1642 edition and taken it home a few months later along with the commentary.

beauty', and several times he compliments the unknown author on his solid head and generous heart, on his smartness, his learning and his flights of fancy. Some of his commendations, however, have an ironical undertone, and it is clear that he considers Browne presumptuous in his speculations, whether religious, metaphysical or scientific.

The autobiographical element in *Religio Medici* seems to have amused Sir Kenelm Digby, but he deplored it as irrelevant to what he took to be the main purpose of the author:

> What should I say of his making so particular a narrative of personall things, and private thoughts of his owne; the knowledge whereof cannot much conduce to any mans betterment? (which I account is the chiefe end of his writing this discourse). And when he speaketh of the soundnesse of his body, of the course of his dyet, of the coolenesse of his blood at the Summer Solstice, of his neglect of an *Epitaph*: how long he hath lived or may live, what *Popes, Emperours, Kings, Grand Seigniors,* he hath been contemporary unto, and the like: would it not be thought that hee hath a speciall good opinion of himselfe (and indeed hee hath reason) when he maketh such great *Princes* the Landmarkes in the Chronology of himselfe? Surely if hee were to write by retaile the particulars of his own Story and life, it would be a notable *Romanze*: since he telleth us in one totall summe, it is a continued miracle of thirty yeares. Though he creepeth gently upon us at the first, yet he groweth a Gyant, an *Attlas*, (to use his owne expression) at the last.[1]

The mockery is good-humoured, but it derives from a misunderstanding of Browne's intentions and methods. Digby supposes the book to be didactic in its aim; nor can he repress his amusement that this nobody should so inflate his little personal idiosyncrasies. Autobiography was not, as a *genre*, uncongenial to Digby. He had himself written (though for

[1] *Observations upon Religio Medici*. Occasionally written by Sir Kenelme Digby, Knight, 1643, p. 53.

private consumption) 'a notable Romanze' about the years of courtship and travel that culminated in his marriage with the beautiful and notorious Venetia Stanley. In a style that recalls Sidney's *Arcadia*, and with a great display of fancy, the story is acted out by characters with fictitious names, and by means of it Digby defends Venetia's essential worth and his own honour. But this was allegorical and romanticised autobiography; moreover, it concerned itself with famous people.

What Sir Kenelm seems to ignore in *Religio Medici* is Browne's contention that any man who will be at pains to anatomise himself can give to his readers a picture that is necessarily unique, yet not singular or unrelated to larger human issues. What can contribute more to an understanding of Man than the records and confessions of individuals? Nor do we need only the records of the exceptionally distinguished; obscurity of situation need be no handicap to self-scrutiny; the one thing absolutely requisite is integrity.

It is Browne's vivid sense of his own uniqueness that dictates the personal reminiscences that we find throughout *Religio Medici*; it is this that unifies all his speculations.

> That world which I regard is my selfe; it is the Microcosme of mine owne frame that I cast mine eye on; for the other, I use it but like my Globe, and turne it round sometimes for my recreation. Men that look upon my outside, perusing onely my condition, and fortunes, do erre in my altitude; for I am above *Atlas* his shoulders, and, though I seeme on earth to stand, on tiptoe in heaven. . . . Whilst I study to finde how I am a Microcosme, or little world, I find myself something more than the great. There is surely a peece of Divinity in us, something that was before the Elements, and owes no homage to the Sun. Nature tels me I am the Image of God as well as Scripture; he that understands not thus much, hath not his introduction or first lesson, and is yet to begin the Alphabet of man.[1]

[1] p. 95 of J. J. Denonain's 1955 edition. All page references are to this edition.

The very structure of the book reveals its free and roving character. Browne is not much concerned, after the first few pages, in defining his religious position; it is the examination of his own vagaries that interests him, though he swings with powerful rhythm from personal to general issues and back again to personal. The progression is not by means of logical argument, but by association; one topic is connected with another by the thread of his fantasy. The final result is an artistically satisfying whole, yet there is something private and arbitrary about the book which gives it its peculiar charm.

To grasp the significance of *Religio Medici* it is necessary to know at what point in Browne's life it was written. In 1634, when the book was drafted, he had just returned to England after three years of study on the Continent, and had not yet taken up the medical practice at Norwich which was to occupy him, together with his scientific and antiquarian studies, for more than forty years until his death in 1682. When he set down the first version of *Religio Medici* Browne was about thirty. He had recently taken his M.D. at Leyden, which at that time had a most distinguished medical school. Previously he had spent a year at Montpellier, where physiological and anatomical studies were flourishing, and another year at Padua, where disciples of Vesalius were encouraging experiments in vivisection. Both in France and Italy the intellectual climate must have been extremely stimulating to a man like Browne, whose interests were both scientific and religious. Montpellier was a half-Catholic, half-Protestant town; Padua, in the Venetian Republic, was secure from Papal interference, and the university was indeed hostile towards the Vatican and the Jesuits. The atmosphere of freedom for discussion and experiment, of tolerance for other men's opinions and customs, decisively affected Browne, who on his return to England was far more interested in the conflict, just reaching definition, between science and religion than in the sectarian and political issues that were preoccupying most of his country-men.

Before his foreign travels Browne had received a very thorough English education. After the death of his father, a London mercer, and the remarriage of his mother, young Thomas was awarded a scholarship in 'Wykeham's School in Winchester', but he failed to get a scholarship to New College, and in 1623 matriculated at Broadgates Hall, subsequently Pembroke College, Oxford. There he spent six years, studying physic, anatomy and botany, besides mastering Latin and Greek and several other languages; he also underwent the usual training in logic and rhetoric, divinity and scholastic philo-sophy. After a brief medical apprenticeship in Oxfordshire and a visit to Ireland, he embarked on his scholar's tour of the Continent.

By the time that he came to write *Religio Medici*, Thomas Browne was a highly educated and cultivated man, well grounded in traditional learning but acquainted too with the best of modern continental thought. His mind was still flexible and receptive, but sufficiently mature to have con-sidered most of the important questions that were then being propounded, and he had arrived at his own conclusions.

In *Religio Medici* he set down his opinions on a vast range of topics—religious belief, the scientific search for truth, the nature of the soul, the creation of the world, the influence of the stars on the destiny of men, angels and devils, witches and oracles, the interpretation of the Bible and a multiplicity of other problems. He did not do this in order to enlighten or edify other men. The book was not intended for publica-tion. It was meant to be, Browne tells us in the preface to the first authorised edition, 'a private exercise directed to my selfe . . . a memorial unto mee . . .', that is to say, a kind

of stocktaking, a summing-up, an attempt to chart his position, intellectual and spiritual, at this important moment of
his life, when his long years of study were over and he was
preparing to embark on the active life of a physician.

Because it touches on so many topics of perennial interest,
religious, scientific and metaphysical, *Religio Medici* has wider
dimensions than the normal essay in autobiography. To some
extent, however, it is a self-portrait, an attempt to delineate
the mind and heart of a sensitive, learned and thoughtful man.

It differs from the majority of self-analytical writings in
being more concerned with opinions and beliefs than with
actions and motives. The mental life is of paramount importance to Browne, and the physical details that he gives about
himself are surprisingly few for a doctor and natural scientist.
Though he alludes more than once to his horoscope, he makes
no reference, such as we might expect from a trained physician,
to his ancestry, or to inherited characteristics, or to the influence
of his early upbringing. Montaigne is far more informative on
these vitally important topics than Browne; and a comparison
with the Italian doctor, Girolamo Cardano, clearly shows
Browne's disregard for the scientific approach to the problem
of individuality. Later he was to read Cardano's *De Vita
Propria Liber*, for he refers to it in *Urn Burial* with a touch of
disparagement. Whereas the Milanese took a clinical interest
in his own body and mind, Browne approached the miracle
of himself with the lens of a poetic imagination.

Had he fulfilled Sir Kenelm Digby's desire and written
'his own Story and life', it would indeed have been a 'notable
Romanze', and something very different from what he did
write, for there is no sustained narrative in *Religio Medici*. The
whole texture of the book is meditative, and most of the
autobiographical detail is conveyed obliquely. It is only by
passing references to foreign customs and to people whom he

has met in France and Italy that we learn of his residence abroad; he does not so much as mention Winchester or Oxford. Yet fragmentary as the personal details are, they are intrinsic to the purpose and structure of *Religio Medici*.

The book is exploratory, not explanatory. In it Browne seeks to relate his intellectual convictions and doubts to his whole personality, and therefore he frequently supplements the record of his considered opinions by vivid instances of his actual behaviour. For him, it is insufficient to say, 'I am, I confess, naturally inclined to that which misguided Zeal terms Superstition.' He proceeds to illustrate this point by contrasting his manners as a citizen with his demeanour as a worshipper:

> My common conversation I do acknowledge austere, my behaviour full of rigour, sometimes not without morosity; yet at my devotion I love to use the civility of my knee, my hat, and hand, with all those outward and sensible motions, which may expresse, or promote my invisible devotion. (p. 7)

These personal details are far more numerous in the second part of *Religio Medici* than in the first; understandably so, since Browne begins by anatomising his beliefs and then proceeds to analyse his disposition. Considerations of faith and hope dominate the first section, reflections on charity the second.

The impression of Sir Thomas Browne which we get from this book derives not only from the information about himself which he deliberately imparts, but also from the manner in which it is conveyed. He is not endeavouring to produce an idealised portrait for his own posterity or for a reading public; when he wrote the book he was still unmarried, and he was an unknown man. *Religio Medici* is wholly free from the self-importance and the considered reticences that characterise Gibbon's *Autobiography*. Browne's attitude towards himself is a compound of patience, curiosity and affection. Although his method is extremely discursive, he accumulates a sufficient number of telling details to make a coherent, rich and solid self-portrait. Many things that we should like to know are ignored, because he was writing primarily for himself; but the private and informal nature of the book enabled him to look at himself steadily and without prejudice.

Whether he or his pirating publisher was responsible for choosing the title, *Religio Medici* indicates well enough the main and explicit theme of the little treatise; but the complexities of his religious attitude are constantly illuminated by what he reveals of his general temper and tastes. That he should be at once devout and sceptical may appear paradoxical at the outset, but we finally have learnt so much about his whole disposition that we return with greater sympathy and understanding to the first part of the book.

One of the first points that Browne notes in *Religio Medici* is his toleration for the religious beliefs of others, extending beyond Christians of differing allegiances to Jews, Turks, infidels and heretics. Such toleration, unusual enough in a seventeenth-century Englishman to be genuinely noteworthy, is later seen to be as much a matter of constitution as of intellectual conviction. Browne explains that he is so naturally sympathetic and acquiescent that he scarcely knows what it is to feel a strong antipathy. He can eat the oddest foreign foods without disgust, he has no horror of noxious creatures, no prejudice against men of other nationalities. Wherever he goes, he carries with him his own serenity. 'I am no Plant that will not prosper out of a Garden. All places, all ayres, make unto me one Country; I am in *England* every where, and under any meridian.' (p. 76)

This sounds perilously like a declaration of insularity; there are many travellers of whom it is only too true that they are in England wherever they may go; yet no reader of *Religio Medici* could accuse Browne of rigidity or of undue Anglophilia. Having travelled with an open and enquiring mind, he returned the better able to appreciate the advantages enjoyed by his own country, especially in matters of religious freedom. There might be rigorists in the Church of England, on both wings, but it was not a persecuting Church, and its very lack of doctrinal definiteness was something that endeared it to Browne. His constitutional tolerance found its spiritual atmosphere congenial; it seemed to him more reasonable in its tenets and demands than any other he had encountered; and he reserved to himself the right of private judgement concerning points of doctrine on which neither Bible nor Church gave any guidance.

After three hundred years, Browne's divagations from orthodoxy have acquired an antiquated charm, whereas the fundamental devoutness of his attitude is inescapably clear. *Religio Medici*, however, did not strike its first readers by the piety of its tone but rather by the free spirit of enquiry which its author exercised in religious and metaphysical matters.

The temper of the preface which Browne wrote for the 1643 edition is extremely defensive and deprecatory. He explains that the book had been composed for his own satisfaction some seven years previously, and it had not been his design to publish it at all; the manuscript, however, had been shown first to one friend, then to another; it had circulated in transcription,[1] and had finally been printed 'most imperfectly and surreptitiously'. The authorised edition contains many corrections, excisions and additions, the changes being motivated by an evident wish to give the little treatise a more

[1] Eight different manuscript versions, none of them in Browne's handwriting, are extant; and none is the immediate source of the 1643 authorised edition. For the fascinating bibliographical background of the book, see J. J. Denonain's 1953 edition.

literary, dignified and orthodox tone. In his preface Browne appears to be genuinely disturbed at the making public of a book intended for his own private benefit. The judicious reader will, he hopes, easily discern that 'what is delivered therein, was rather a memorial unto mee, than an Example, or Rule, to any other'. Foreseeing that the book will be misunderstood and misrepresented, he pleads that it belongs to his younger years and does not necessarily mirror his present opinions; moreover, it is composed in a rhetorical or figurative style, so that not everything in it should be 'called unto the rigid test of Reason'.

This apologetic preface did not save Browne from being severely and systematically taken to task by that puritanical know-all, Alexander Ross, in *Medicus Medicatus, or the Physicians Religion Cured by a Lenitive or Gentle Potion*. Considered as the product of an age in which no controversial holds were barred, it may be admitted that Ross's pamphlet is comparatively mild; he acknowledges as a point in Browne's favour his readiness to defer to maturer judgements; but he chides him sharply for every deviation from the straight and narrow path of scriptural Christianity. Occasionally, among his moral and doctrinal reproofs, Ross scores a good point:

> You thank God, you have escaped pride, the mortall enemy to charity. So did the Pharisee thank God, that hee was no extortioner; yet hee went home unjustified. *Pride* is a more subtle sin than you conceive; it thrusts itself upon our best actions . . . and have you not pride, in thinking you have no pride?[1]

Only at the end of his discourse does Ross acknowledge that there is 'much worth and good language' in *Religio Medici*; and even then he makes it clear that he really regards the style as insidious, for he goes on to remark that he has taken the trouble

[1] *Medicus Medicatus*, 1645, p. 73.

(busy man though he is, with many more important matters to occupy him) to refute Browne's errors

> to let green heads and inconsiderate young Gentlemen see, that there is some danger in reading your Book, without the *spectacles* of judgment, for, whilst they are taken with the gilding of your phrase, they may swallow unaware such *pills*, as may rather kill then cure them.[1]

One thinks again of the seventeen-year-old John Aubrey's delight in the book that first opened his understanding.

Religio Medici made a great sensation when it was issued, appearing in two Latin editions in the year following its authorised publication in England, and being translated during the author's lifetime into French, German and Dutch.[2] Critics at the time were not at all sure how to take it, and indeed it is a work that almost defies classification; it is a good deal easier to say what it is not than to describe it in positive terms. What amazed, and sometimes scandalised, Browne's contemporaries was the quiet, almost nonchalant way in which he expressed his judgements upon highly controversial matters. It was because he, a layman with a scientific training, elected to write about religious beliefs that the book seemed so momentous. Some of his critics, like Guy Patin, the French experimental philosopher, admired his freedom from bigotry; others thought his open-mindedness subversive; all considered *Religio Medici* a challenging piece of work, because of its liberal and speculative temper.

[1] *Medicus Medicatus*, 1645, p. 80. Ross, not content with rebuking Browne, also published *Animadversions* on the *Observations* of Sir Kenelm Digby. In 1652 he snatched a little time from his inept continuation of Raleigh's *History of the World* to write *Arcana Microcosmi*, a stout defence of Aristotelian physiology against the Galenists, together with 'A Refutation of Doctor Browne's Vulgar Errors, the Lord Bacon's Natural History, and Doctor Harvy's Book De Generatione.'

[2] By 1686, when Browne's *Complete Works* were published, four years after his death, the English editions numbered ten.

The average educated man of the seventeenth century was prepared to test Browne's theorising, whether about the nature of the soul or the locality of hell or the salvation of those who lived in pre-Christian times, by reference to specific theological and metaphysical tenets in a way that today astonishes us by its precision. It was Coleridge who pointed out that they were barking up the wrong tree. Of Sir Kenelm Digby's *Observations* he remarked:

> He ought to have considered the *Religio Medici* in a dramatic, and not in a metaphysical view, as a sweet exhibition of character and passion, and not as an expression, or investigation, of positive truth. The *Religio Medici* is a fine portrait of a handsome man in his best clothes.[1]

Actually the outward features, the best clothes, are not much in evidence, although the artist is well disposed towards his subject and usually places him in the best light; for the inner man, spiritual and intellectual, is Browne's real preoccupation. Moreover, as has been already said, the wide range of topics covered in the book makes it something more complex than an essay in autobiography. Yet Coleridge was right; only if we approach *Religio Medici* as a piece of self-revelation can we rightly appreciate Browne's handling of intellectual problems.

There are some apparent contradictions in Browne's self-portrait. Though he plumes himself on his tolerance, benevolence and lack of pride, he despises the Multitude: '. . . that great enemy of reason, vertue and religion . . . that numerous piece of monstrosity, which taken asunder seem men, and reasonable creatures of God; but confused together, make but one great beast . . .' (p. 76) His reason for contempt, however, is a sound one, based upon the perception that men collectively act more brutishly and basely than they do as

---

[1] *Notes on Sir Thomas Browne's Religio Medici*, 1802. Reprinted in *Miscellaneous Criticism of S. T. Coleridge*, ed. T. M. Raysor, 1936, p. 252.

individuals. He claims to converse with all men, making no more distinction between good and bad than the sun does, and with a friendly aspect to everyone; yet he admits to austerity and even moroseness of demeanour. We get the impression of an acutely sensitive man, gentle, meditative, sometimes genuinely afraid to be alone with himself:

> It is the corruption that I feare within me, not the contagion of commerce without me. 'Tis that unruly regiment within me, that will destroy me, 'tis I that doe infect my selfe . . . therefore . . . Lord, deliver me from my selfe, is a part of my Letany, and the first voice of my retired imaginations. . . . Indeed, though in a Wildernesse, a man is never alone, not onely because hee is with himselfe, and his owne thoughts, but because he is with the devill, who ever consorts with our solitude, and is that unruly rebell that musters up those disordered motions, which accompany our sequestred imaginations. . . . (p. 94)

Here is a consciousness of inner disharmony that is as acute as any expressed by Donne; and Browne's awareness of his own human frailty and inadequacy has brought him sometimes, he confesses, to the point of contemplating suicide. It is not the burden of unconfessed transgressions, or the commission of vicious and villainous acts (for which, he says, he was always too unenterprising) that torments him:

> Those common and quotidian informities that so necessarily attend me, and doe seeme to bee my very nature, have so dejected me, so broken the estimation that I should have otherwise of my selfe, that I repute my selfe the most abjectest piece of mortality, that I detest my owne nature, and in my retired imaginations cannot withhold my hands from violence on my selfe. . . .[1]

Life is tolerable only because death puts a term to it. Already in *Religio Medici* we can see Browne's preoccupation

[1] p. 88. Prof. Denonain has restored the last two clauses from a manuscript version; they do not appear in the 1643 edition.

with the theme that was in later years to move him to his most magnificent flights of eloquence. He treats it here a great deal less rhetorically than in *Hydriotaphia*, aware that his own death-wish is dangerously strong. In the 1643 edition he is at pains to show that he regards the prospect of death with equanimity and courage:

> In expectation of a better, I can with patience embrace this life, yet in my best meditations do often defie death; I honour any man that contemns it, nor can I highly love any that is afraid of it: this makes me naturally love a Souldier, and honour those tattered and contemptible Regiments that will die at the command of a Sergeant.[1]

In the text as restored by Professor Denonain, the passage about the soldiers is preceded by some very different considerations:

> In expectation of a better, I can with patience embrace this life, yet in my best meditations doe often desire death; It is a sympton of melancholy to be afraid of death, yet sometimes to desire it; this latter I have often discovered in my selfe, and thinke no man ever desired life, as I have sometimes death. (p. 51)

The thought of dying, then, inspires in him no fear, but the indignities of corruption rouse his sense of shame. His anatomical and medical studies have familiarised him with the physical horrors of death, though without hardening him. The experience of dissecting-rooms and mortuaries lies behind his account of how, during a storm at sea, he was reconciled to the prospect of drowning by the thought of the ignominy of becoming a corpse, subjected to 'wondering eyes, tears of pity, lectures of mortality'. Not, he adds with a touch of sardonic humour,

> that I am ashamed of the Anatomy of my parts, or can accuse nature for playing the bungler in any part of me, or my owne

---

[1] *Religio Medici*, Everyman's Library, p. 44.

vitious life for contracting any shamefull disease upon me, whereby I might not call my selfe as wholesome a morsell for the wormes as any. (p. 53)

Again and again we are reminded that a doctor is writing these disquisitions on the value of human life, as when he reflects:

Men that looke no further than their outsides, thinke health an appertinance unto life, and quarrell with their constitutions for being sick; but I that have examined the parts of man, and know upon what tender filaments that Fabrick hangs, doe wonder that we are not alwayes so; and considering the thousand dores that lead to death doe thank my God that we can die but once. (p. 57)

No passage in the book is more directly autobiographical, or more amusing, than the eighth section of the second part, in which Browne congratulates himself on having escaped the sin of pride. That he never thrust himself forward or boasted of his accomplishments we may well believe; that he privately underestimated his own worth seems less probable.

For my owne part, besides the *Jargon* and *Patois* of severall Provinces, I understand no lesse than six Languages, yet I protest I have no higher conceit of my selfe, than had our Fathers before the confusion of *Babel*, when there was in the world but one Language, and none to boast himselfe either Linguist or Criticke. I have not onely seene severall Countries, beheld the nature of their climes, the Chorography of their Provinces, Topography of their Cities, but understand their severall Lawes, Customes and Policies; yet cannot all this perswade the dulnesse of my spirit unto such an opinion of my self, as I behold in nimbler and conceited heads, that never looked a degree beyond their nests. I know the names, and somewhat more, of all the constellations in my Horizon, yet I have seene a prating Mariner, that could onely name the Poynters and the North Starre, out-talke mee, and conceit himselfe a whole Spheare above mee. (p. 89)

People who talked big invited Browne's contempt; his

own manner must have been quiet and subdued, the natural reflection of his melancholy temperament. 'I am naturally bashful; nor hath conversation, age, or travel, been able to effront or enharden me. . . .' (p. 53) To this innate modesty he attributes his shame at the thought of death's corruption, and perhaps it is also ultimately responsible for his comment on the act of sexual intercourse:

> I could be content that we might procreate like trees, without conjunction, or that there were any way to perpetuate the world without this triviall and vulgar way of coition; it is the foolishest act a wise man commits in all his life, nor is there any thing that will more deject his coold imagination, when hee shall consider what an odde and unworthy piece of folly hee hath committed. . . . (p. 91)

Religio Medici was written before Browne had entered on a thoroughly happy marriage, and his frigid and pedantic remarks on a man's relationship to his wife and children belong rather to the moralising Senecan tradition of essay-writing than to the man who was to father twelve children and in later life to write such delightful letters to his sons, with enchantingly ill-spelt postscripts added by their devoted mother. So, too, the disquisition on friendship; it bears no personal stamp. When, however, he talks of dreams—another popular topic with essayists—he relates the astrological details of his nativity, and by a vivid touch of reminiscence takes us unexpectedly quite into his confidence:

> At my Nativity, my ascendant was the watery signe of *Scorpius*; I was borne in the Planetary hour of *Saturne*, and I think I have a peece of that Leaden Planet in me. I am no way facetious, nor disposed for the mirth and galliardize of company, yet in one dreame I can compose a whole comedy, behold the action, apprehend the jests, and laugh my selfe awake at the conceits thereof. . . . (p. 96)

Writing of music, he is led into metaphysical fancies of great beauty, but here too there are homely and topical touches which have the authentically autobiographical ring about them:

> Whosoever is harmonically composed delights in harmony; which makes me much mistrust the symmetry of those heads which declaime against all Church musicke. For my selfe, not only from my obedience, but my particular genius, I do embrace it: for even that vulgar and Taverne Musicke, which makes one man merry, another mad, strikes mee into a deepe fit of devotion, and a profound contemplation of the first Composer; there is something of Divinity in it more than the eare discovers. (p. 91)

This completely natural and unforced quickening of the spirit of devotion is extremely characteristic of Browne's reaction to experience. He was a man who worshipped almost instinctively; a man whose overmastering spirit of wonder impelled him both to thank God for His wisdom and mercy and to speculate about the works of His creation.

Religio Medici is pervaded by a temper of humble thankfulness. There is no personal devotion to Christ manifested in its pages, but as complete an acceptance of the providence and wisdom of God as can be found in the writings of Jeremy Taylor or George Herbert. Acknowledging his incapacity to penetrate the mysteries of religion, Browne rejoices that these mysteries exist and that a man is required to exercise faith as well as reason in the pursuit of truth. The book ends with a profoundly Christian prayer:

> Dispose of me according to the wisedome of thy pleasure. Thy will bee done, though in my owne undoing. (p. 102)

The reader is not left with any sense of incongruity between this expression of devout humility and the general trend of the book; Browne's religious certainties far outweigh his doubts and speculations.

He differed from many of his pious contemporaries in not being tormented by a grievous and gnawing sense of sin. It is true that when he speaks of the inner conflicts of his spirit he is moved to use language of poetic intensity: 'The heart of man is the place the devill dwels in; I feele sometimes a hell within my selfe, *Lucifer* keeps his court in my brest, *Legion* is revived in me.' (p. 67) Or, again,

> Let mee be nothing, if within the compasse of my selfe, I doe not find the battle of *Lepanto*, passion against reason, reason against faith, faith against the Devill, and my Conscience against all. There is another man within mee that's angry with mee, rebukes, commands, and dastards mee. (p. 87)

He does not minimise the human propensity to err, nor under-rate the risk of damnation; yet his natural benevolence makes him insist that the extent of God's love and saving mercy cannot be limited by the presumptions of uncharitable sectarians; and as far as he himself is concerned, he confesses that he was never afraid of Hell, and he despises terror as a religious weapon. 'I can hardly thinke there was ever any scared into Heaven; they go the surest way to Heaven who would serve God without a Hell.' (p. 68)

Surveying the course of his life, Browne perceives only 'an abysse and masse of God's mercies, either in generall to mankind or in particular to my selfe'. Lest this should seem merely facile complacence, he explains that what others term 'Crosses, afflictions, judgements, misfortunes, to me who enquire further into them than their visible effects they both appeare, and in event have ever proved, the secret and dissembled favours of his affection.' (p. 68) This is the same thorough-going acceptance of the goodness and wisdom of God, no matter how displayed, as animates the prayer with which Browne concludes his book.

This genuine piety was linked with a reverence for traditional religious observances, and it was fortunate for Browne that he found in the Anglican church of his day an institution squaring with his conscience, consonant to his reason, and framed to his particular devotion. He comments upon the apparent contrast between his daring in speculation and his submissive attitude in religion, but evidently feels no need to justify any inconsistency; his mind and spirit were so poised that they required and enjoyed both liberty and obedience. 'In Philosophy where truth seemes double-faced, there is no man more paradoxicall then my selfe: but in Divinity I love to keepe the road, and, though not in an implicite, yet an humble faith, follow the great wheele of the Church. . . .' (p. 10)

Browne's scientific curiosity was not in the least at variance with his religious devotion. The same sense of wonder which impelled him to worship incited him also to a study of natural phenomena.

> The wisedome of God receives small honour from those vulgar heads that rudely stare about, and with a grosse rusticity admire his workes; those highly magnifie him, whose judicious enquiry into his acts, and deliberate research of his creatures, returne the duty of a devout and learned admiration. (p. 19)

In the marvels of the created world he saw testimony to the wisdom of God, and he considered natural science in no way inferior to the study of the Scriptures as a means for arriving at a knowledge of the Creator's omniscience and omnipotence. There is an implied criticism of medieval scholastic learning in the following passage, with its insistence on the superior kind of curiosity manifested by the Greeks and Romans:

> Thus there are two bookes from whence I collect my Divinity; besides that one written of God, another of his servant Nature,

that universall and publik Manuscript, that lives expans'd unto
the eyes of all: those that never saw him in the one, have discovered him in the other. . . . Surely the Heathens knew better
how to joyne and reade these mysticall letters than wee Christians,
who cast a more careless eye on these common Hieroglyphicks,
and disdain to suck Divinity from the flowers of nature. (p. 21)

In subsequent years, while most of his countrymen were
engaged in fierce sectarian and political strife, Browne quietly
pursued his studies of natural history, folk-lore and archaeology.
In 1646 he published *Pseudodoxia Epidemica, or Enquiries into
very many received tenets and commonly-presumed truths, which
examined prove but Vulgar and Common Errors.* His paper about
sepulchral urns recently found in Norfolk was published in
1658, and as *Hydriotaphia or Urn Burial* secured a place in
English literature quite unparalleled by any little local treatise
compiled by a country doctor in his spare time. To the end of
his life he corresponded with celebrated antiquarians, including
Sir William Dugdale, John Evelyn (with whom he shared an
interest in botany, and who visited him at his Norwich home
in 1671), Elias Ashmole, and even with John Aubrey, his young
admirer now grown middle-aged. He made notes for a natural
history of Norfolk and East Anglia, and his correspondence
with Henry Oldenburg proves his wish to serve the Royal
Society. His son Edward, a less distinguished man than his
father, was elected a member of this illustrious body, and we
may wonder why Browne himself was not invited to join it at
its inception. The answer probably lies in the vein of fantasy
that often dictates his approach to knowledge and continually is
mirrored in his style. His omnivorous, amateurish kind of
learning became antiquated within his own span of life, and his
magniloquence did not in the least conform to the standards of
prose laid down for members of the Royal Society, who were
recommended to express themselves in a close, naked, natural

way of speaking, positively, clearly and with a native easiness. But *Religio Medici*, a little private treatise, has acquired the significance of a monument for the very reason that it preserves a type of electicism that did not and could not reappear in England after the Restoration. Written at the very end of a great cultural epoch by a man with a vast command of imaginative eloquence, the book perpetuates a moment of poise between the traditional Christian past and the expanding scientific future.

Browne's medical studies, his travels, his contacts with sceptical minds at foreign universities and his wide reading all reinforced his persuasion that Man is a creature of immense complexity: 'I find there are many pieces in this one fabrick of man; this frame is raised upon a masse of Antipathies.' (p. 87) He remarks that the whole creation is a mystery, and man the most mysterious unit within it, and therefore the most worthy of study. The science of man, in Browne's day, involved also the study of stars and planetary signs, the elements and humours; among his correspondents were more than one astrologer. But, as a medical man, when he speaks of the study of man he primarily means research into the functioning of his physical and psychical being, along the bold experimental lines that he had seen at Montpellier and Padua. Of the importance of self-study he also speaks unequivocally. The summit of God's wisdom, he says, 'is in comprehending that he made not, that is himselfe. And this also is the greatest knowledge in man.' (p. 18)

Religio Medici is to some extent an essay in self-knowledge, and it is redeemed from any taint of egocentricity by the conviction pervading the whole book, that every individual is inextricably involved in mankind.

I could never content my contemplation with those generall pieces of wonder, the flux and reflux of the Sea, the encrease of

Nile, the conversion of the Needle to the North, and therefore have studied to match and parallel these in the more obvious and neglected pieces of Nature, which without further travell I can doe in the Cosmography of my selfe; wee carry with us the wonders we seeke without us: There is all *Africa* and her prodigies in us; we are that bold and adventurous piece of nature, which he that studies wisely learns in a *compendium* what others labour at in a divided piece and endless volume. (p. 21)

This recalls the plea of Sir John Davies, that discoverers should not be content with navigating the world but should apply their energies to the study of their own individualities. Browne's quest was less purely metaphysical than that of Davies, for what he especially hoped for was an extension of knowledge about human nature that should be based upon the study of human anatomy and physiology; but at the same time, he was possessed by the fascination of self-examination. His bent for introspection had made it quite clear to him that the individual mind is inadequate to the task of comprehending itself; and this sense of the finiteness and fallibility of his own judgement underlies the extreme tolerance which he shows towards other men's opinions and their behaviour.

No man can justly censure or condemne another, because indeed no man truely knows another. This I perceive in my selfe, for I am in the darke to all the world, and my nearest friends behold mee but in a cloud; those that know mee superficially, thinke lesse of me than I doe of my selfe; those of my neere acquaintance thinke more. . . . Further, no man can judge another, because no man knowes himselfe, for we censure others but as they disagree from that humour which wee fancy laudable in our selves, and commend them but for that wherein they seeme to quadrate and consent with us. . . . (p. 82)

In this tolerance and refusal to judge his fellows, Browne resembles Montaigne. His inability to take controversies seriously springs from the same attitude as prompted Montaigne's *Que scais-je?* 'I could never divide my selfe from any man upon the difference of an opinion, or be angry with his judgement for not agreeing with mee in that, from which perhaps within a few dayes I should dissent my selfe.' (p. 9) But Browne's tolerance, like his scepticism, is comprehended within the larger compass of his religious feeling. Here there is a very great difference between the two men. Montaigne was outwardly pious, and died fortified by the rites of Holy Church, in spite of all that he had done to cut away the foundations of religious belief. Browne was genuinely religious. More than *Christian Morals*, that edifying but somewhat sententious work of his later years, *Religio Medici* is the testament of a worshipping man.

Browne's debt to Montaigne remains imponderable. The similarities in spirit and in approach have been observed by many critics; yet one can only say that he assimilated from the *Essais* whatever was congenial to his own temperament. It is not primarily a stylistic debt, for though his relaxed and familiar manner is reminiscent of Montaigne, Browne can be as impassioned as Donne; moreover, *Religio Medici* is singularly free from bookish allusions, thanks to the lucky chance that it was written when he was far from his library.

One of the greatest delights of *Religio Medici* is its variety of tone, ranging from that of easy and familiar conversation to the highest flights of imaginative rhetoric. By the very flexibility of his style and manner, Browne effectively acquaints us with himself and at the same time reminds us that the whole of mankind is, in Montaigne's phrase, 'merveilleusement vain, divers et ondoyant'. Whimsical the book may be, but only because the man himself was constitutionally whimsical. He was not a practised writer when he committed to paper these personal reflections of life and death, on human nature and behaviour and on his own individuality. Because they were originally intended for private consumption, there is no deliberate cultivation of the 'gentle reader', although the authorised version of 1643 is rather less informal than the earlier drafts. In later years, Browne did cultivate with considerable care a solemn and sonorous style and could be fairly accused of literary self-consciousness,[1] but in this private 'memorial', we merely overhear his meditations and sometimes his reminiscences.

When his topic is sublime, his language soars, his cadences become splendid; but he can equally well employ homely words and forceful phrases, when the occasion calls for them. *Religio Medici* is not a studied, polished, mannered piece of literary prose—some of it is almost slovenly in style; but it has a livelier charm than *Hydriotaphia* or *The Garden of Cyrus*, partly because its subject matter is infinitely more varied, partly because of its stylistic spontaneity.

Browne's variability of manner was not lost upon his first critic, Sir Kenelm Digby, who commented:

> I would enquire (especially upon his suddaine poeticall rapture) whether the solidity of the *Judgement* bee not sometimes outweighed by the ayriness of the fancy. Assuredly one cannot erre in taking this Author for a very fine ingenious Gentleman: but for how deepe a *Scholler*, I leave unto them to judge, that are abler then I am. (*Observations*, p. 38)

Here Digby, who had censured the work for failing to be a systematic philosophical treatise, stumbles upon the truth that it is an imaginative creation, the product of a poetic mind.

The true value of *Religio Medici* as an autobiography depends upon its intrinsically poetic quality; a poetry expressed in the variegated texture of the style, but deriving from

[1] See Gilbert Phelps, 'The Prose of Donne and Browne', in *From Donne to Marvell*, Penguin, 1956.

Browne's imaginative approach to himself and to human nature. We learn from its pages very few verifiable facts about its author, but we cannot read it without adding the name of Sir Thomas Browne to the list of the people with whom we are genuinely familiar. By oblique methods he achieved an authentic self-portrait. It was not through aiming at precision and veracity of detail that he accomplished it, but by seeing his life as 'a miracle of thirty yeares . . . a piece of poetry'.

Most autobiographies belong to the category of history, and the mental faculty most active in their production is the memory; but *Religio Medici* belongs to the literature of the imagination. Memory has had little to do with its compilation; not the past, but the present, is Browne's concern. Like an impressionist painter, he attempts to capture truth in its very transience. What he is now at this moment, with all his quirks and quiddities of opinion and behaviour—this it is that interests him even more than the problem of how and why he came to be the man he is.

Montaigne knew what a formidably difficult task it is for a writer to discover and express his true, elusive identity:

> 'Tis a rugged road, more so than it seems, to follow a pace so rambling and uncertain, as that of the soul; to penetrate the dark profundities of its intricate internal windings, to choose and lay hold of so many little nimble motions; 'tis a new and extraordinary undertaking. . . .

Browne's thorough understanding of this problem is reflected in the very elasticity of the structure and language of *Religio Medici*. As though he perceived that truth must be taken unawares, by devious and original approaches, he avoids everything that is rigid or systematic. The mere facts of his earthly existence, did he care to assemble them, would amount to no more than a *dossier*, a clinical case-history. They would be insufficient to account for what he actually is, a sentient, thinking, human being, uniquely himself. To measure his own significance, Browne's eye, like the true poet's, 'doth move from heaven to earth, from earth to heaven'. Only so can he hope to suggest the mystery that surrounds his life, as it surrounds the life of every single individual.

Lord Herbert of Cherbury

❧

The appreciation of an autobiography should be based upon the concept of the man and the mask, the private and the public face; for if, in daily life, the give-away gesture and the characteristic evasion are clues by which we recognise the psychic duality of our fellows, they are even more significant in a man's considered account of his own life. He may consciously aim at veracity, and yet he will be betrayed by that tendency to self-deception which Pascal noted in too bitter terms—'Man is only disguise, falsehood and hypocrisy, both in himself and in regard to others.'

No autobiography raises this issue of 'disguise' more sharply than that written by Lord Herbert of Cherbury, about the year 1643. He was by that time a man of sixty, ailing, harassed by a Civil War in which he played an unwilling and inglorious part. Twenty years of frustration separated him from his gay and active heyday of soldiering and diplomacy and amorous adventure. During those twenty years since his recall from the ambassadorship in Paris, he had done distinguished work as a philosopher and historian, and in his retirement at Montgomery Castle had had plenty of leisure to ponder on the changes and chances of this mortal life. When he set himself to write his autobiography, he had, explicitly, two admirable purposes in mind. The first was to record for his posterity 'those passages of my life, which I conceive may best declare me and be most useful to them'; the second was to recall his past in order that, before it was too late, he might examine himself with a view to repentance, reformation and making his peace with God. However, by the time he had written some fifty pages, he had lost sight of his didactic intention in the sheer pleasure of re-living his golden years; and as for the second motive, there is scarcely an indication in the whole volume that, having once mentioned it, he ever gave it another thought.

What makes the *Autobiography* such a disconcerting book is that the picture presented with such obvious affection and pride by Lord Herbert conveys such an imperfect likeness of the man whom, from his other writings and achievements, we know Lord Herbert to have been. The image of himself that delights him is that of an irresistibly good-looking, quixotically chivalrous, ostentatiously magnificent gentleman; an intrepid man of action, courtier, soldier, traveller, diplomatist. Whatever does not contribute to the enhancement of this image is omitted or played down. Yet Herbert's chief claim to fame rests upon his philosophical treatises, *De Veritate*, *Religio Laici* and *De Religione Gentilium*. It is because of these that he has a secure place in the history of English thought, as 'father of the Deists'. His poetry, too, holds its own with all but the very best of metaphysical verse; nor was he negligible as a historian.

The Autobiography breaks off abruptly at the year 1624, before Herbert had consolidated his serious studies; and he makes it apparent, in the earlier section of the book, that he was a man of learning, a virtuoso with a wide range of interests; but the liveliest, the most spontaneous part of the chronicle is devoted to the recollection of trivial incidents, all ministering rather ridiculously to Lord Herbert's self-esteem. The egregiously conceited tone of the book has given great delight to its admirers, from Horace Walpole onwards. Though self-adulation is a common enough disguise for frustration, it is not at all easy to account for Herbert's principles of selection or his assessment of the relative importance of the many strands of experience that made up his life. Misch in his *History of Autobiography in Antiquity* remarks that the spirit brooding on the recollected material is the truest and most real element in an autobiography. The cleverest liar will give himself away through the very selection of his lies; the truth is revealed by the weight a man places upon seemingly trifling incidents. One can only conclude, after reading Lord Herbert, that his faculties of self-criticism lay dormant, even through his years of disappointment and adversity, and that in old age he was as pleased as he had been in his prime with Edward Herbert, the last of the knights errant.

'I propose to write with all truth and sincerity, as scorning ever to deceive or speak false to any,' says Herbert in his preamble; and he does indeed maintain a tone of frankness that led his discoverer, Horace Walpole, to consider him the incarnation of truthfulness. Sir Sidney Lee, however, was a far more wary editor, and in his introduction to the *Autobiography* he drew the reader's attention to many omissions and inaccuracies.[1] He was, moreover, the first to show, by supplementing Herbert's chronicle with evidence derived from other sources, how misleading, in a strictly historical sense, the old man was. Not that this lack of strict veracity diminishes in the least the charm of the book. Rather, it increases it, for Herbert's blind spots and biases contribute to the expression of that psychological truth which is the essence of every good autobiography.

The book is not, judged as a work of art, a satisfactory creation. Apart from being incomplete, it suffers from being

---

[1] *The Autobiography of Lord Herbert of Cherbury*, with introduction, notes, appendices, and a continuation of the life, by Sidney Lee. First edition, 1886; second, revised, 1906. Page references are to the 2nd ed.

mixed in type. It is not a straightforward memoir, such as was the life-history of Robert Cary, Earl of Monmouth, composed some years previously.[1] This lively work, addressed to nobody in particular, by an eye-witness of the defeat of the Armada and the death of Queen Elizabeth, is the annals of a prominent man of action set in the larger framework of public affairs. Herbert's *Autobiography* does partially belong to this type of personal chronicle, objective in tone and narrative in method; but it also sets out to transmit experience and advice for the benefit of posterity, sometimes in a manner that recalls the Elizabethan courtesy books, sometimes with a semi-scientific detachment that brings Cardano to mind. The opening sections of the book, before Herbert gets into his narrative stride, have not received the attention that they deserve, simply because they are less comic than what follows; but they contribute very much to the interest of the work considered as an experiment in an almost untried literary *genre*.

About the time of the Reformation, a liking for portraiture developed in England. Henry VIII's patronage of Holbein is not unrelated to the beginnings of English biography—lives of individual men presented with an emphasis on personal detail, such as we find in Roper's memorial to his father-in-law, Sir Thomas More, or in Cavendish's *Life of Cardinal Wolsey*. Lord Herbert's originality consists in his concern to give a lively likeness of himself in his autobiography. Although he had been concerned in public affairs, he specifically avoided discussing diplomatic negotiations in his book, 'it being a more perplexed and secret business than I am willing to insert into the narrative of my life.' (p. 131) Other memorialists, like Sir James Melville, an Ambassador of Mary Queen of Scots, subordinate their private affairs to the public events in which they participated. Melville's avowed intention in

[1] *Memoirs of Robert Cary*, ed. G. H. Powell, 1905.

writing his *Memorialis* is to serve for an exemplar of life and better behaviour to his sons 'concerning the service of princes and meddling in their affaires'.[1] Herbert's experience of Stuart ingratitude qualified him to write a cautionary tale, but this he did not do; nor was his choice of incidents for relation really determined by the wish to edify his descendants. Portraiture was what he cared about; not an anatomical study of the old, disappointed man that he had become, but the reconstruction in words of a romantic image of Edward Herbert, like that depicted by Isaac Oliver, in which the strikingly handsome and exquisitely dressed cavalier reclines under a tree, his gauntlet much in evidence and his horses in the middle distance.

It was not until the early eighteenth century that memoirs achieved popularity as a literary form in England. Though many were written during and after the Civil War by notable people who felt constrained by the insecurity of the times to record their personal impressions, these were all intended for family reading. Few have the intimate touch of Lady Fanshawe's enchanting memoirs written for her ten-year-old son; but none were meant for the eyes of strangers, and all existed in private archives as separate manifestations of a widely diffused impulse. Edward Herbert, then, was following no approved model when he set himself to write his autobiography.

The book, after a preamble, begins with an account of Herbert's ancestors, working backward through four generations of the male line, with an abundance of anecdotes about their valour. His mother's family is treated much more briefly, but a good deal is related about Edward's brothers and sisters. It is characteristic that though he speaks with admiration of George, the poet, whose 'life was most holy and exemplary',

[1] *Memoirs of Sir James Melville*, ed. A. Francis Stewart, 1929, p. 1.

the brother on whom he lavishes most attention is Thomas, the youngest, who in the navy kept up the family tradition of intrepidity.

Lord Herbert then gives some account of his own birth and early childhood. He was a sickly baby, and backward in talking, but not, according to his own estimate, at all backward in intelligence, for

> The very furthest thing that I remember, is, that when I understood what was said by others, I did yet forbear to speak, lest I should utter something that were imperfect or impertinent. When I came to talk, one of the furthest enquiries I made was, how I came into this world? (p. 15)

Herbert was enough of a natural scientist to be interested in heredity, and he includes many details about his health. This modern awareness of the importance of the physical constitution makes him break off in the midst of his French adventures to mention that he grew half an inch at the age of thirty-six, that he was light in weight compared with men much slighter and shorter than himself, and that he had a pulse in the crown of his head. Moreover,

> It is well known to these that wait in my chamber, that the shirts, waistcoats and other garments that I wear next my body, are sweet, beyond what either easily can be believed, or hath been observed in any else, which sweetness was also found to be in my breath above others, before I was used to take tobacco, which, towards my latter time, I was forced to take against certain rheums and catarrhs that trouble me, which yet did not taint my breath for any long time; I scarce ever felt cold in my life, though yet so subject to catarrhs, that I think no man was ever more obnoxious to it; all which I do in a familiar way mention to my posterity, though otherwise they might be thought scarcely worth the writing. (p. 113)

Herbert recounts the years of his boyhood under various

tutors, his father's death, his early marriage to an older but well-endowed cousin, his education at Oxford and his removal at the age of eighteen to his mother's house in London, 'between which place and Montgomery Castle I passed my time till I came to the age of one-and-twenty, having in that space divers children'. (p. 23) He then devotes almost as many pages as he has already spent to some general observations on education, 'even from the first infancy till the departure from the University; as being desirous, together with the narration of my life, to deliver such rules as I conceive may be useful to my posterity.' (p. 23)

Although this educational digression owes much to the tradition of the courtesy books—Herbert himself refers to Guazzo and della Casa, and is concerned in the larger sense, like Castiglione or Sir Thomas Elyot, with the training of a gentle-man—his observations throw much light upon his own convictions and tastes. This is the most seriously instructive part of the autobiography, and Herbert brings it to an end with the remark that he intends to make a little treatise about how a gentleman should behave himself with children, servants, tenants and neighbours; an intention that may have been embodied in *A Dialogue between a Tutor and a Pupil*.[1]

After this interlude, the narration of his own history is resumed; and from that point until the book comes to an abrupt stop, the author is thoroughly enjoying himself. With immense relish he recalls all his youthful triumphs, the first of them during his visit to the court of Elizabeth, when the old queen looked attentively upon him and, 'swearing her ordinary oath, said it was a pity he was married so young', twice giving him her hand to kiss, and patting him gently on the cheek. The entertainment value of this part of the *Autobiography* has never been in question; it is written in the most lively and

[1] Published in 1768 and attributed to Herbert.

unaffected way, and the figure presented is extraordinary indeed.

Edward Herbert, created a Knight of the Bath along with some sixty other gentlemen at the accession of James I, chose to regard this not very remarkable distinction as a true accolade. Himself observing that the oaths subscribed to were 'not unlike the romances of knight errantry', he elected to take seriously the rescuing of damsels in distress and the obligation to engage in single combat on every occasion when his honour seemed to be threatened. That he must frequently have made a considerable fool of himself is quite apparent from the stories that he tells, though naturally the folly was imperceptible to him. He was perpetually taking offence and behaving with bravado. However, his good looks and undoubted courage seem to have carried him through his difficulties, and according to his own account he was immensely popular wherever he went, especially with the ladies. He disported himself in France, he fought at the siege of Juliers, he travelled as far afield as Rome, he cut a great dash as ambassador in Paris—and actually carried out his mission there with great sagacity, though from the autobiography we could scarcely suspect him of the good judgement that history shows him to have exercised. He also, in his spare time, wrote poems, which are not mentioned at all, and *De Veritate*, of which he writes most engagingly.

The book, an enquiry into the nature of truth and the means of apprehending it, had been begun in England and finished in Paris—'all the spare hours, which I could get from my visits and negotiations, being employed to perfect this work'. (p. 132) Herbert submitted it to Grotius and Tilenus, and the hearty commendation of these great scholars encouraged him to think of publication; but he was well aware of the book's unorthodoxy, and guessed that his treatment of revealed truth would arouse strong opposition, so that he thought of suppressing it for a while. Being thus doubtful, he acted in a way which beautifully reveals the complexity of his character.

Being thus doubtful in my chamber, one fair day in the summer, my casement being opened towards the south, the sun shining clear, and no wind stirring, I took my book, *De Veritate*, in my hand, and, and, kneeling on my knees, devoutly said these words: 'O thou eternal God, Author of the light which now shines upon me, and Giver of all inward illuminations, I do beseech Thee, of Thy infinite goodness, to pardon a greater request than a sinner ought to make; I am not satisfied enough whether I shall publish this Book, *De Veritate*; if it be for Thy glory, I beseech Thee, give me some sign from heaven; if not, I shall suppress it.' I had no sooner spoken these words, but a loud though gentle noise came from the heavens, for it was like nothing on earth, which did so comfort and cheer me, that I took my petition as granted, and that I had the sign I demanded, whereupon also I resolved to print my book. This, how strange soever it may seem, I protest before the eternal God is true, neither am I in any way superstitiously deceived herein, since I did not only clearly hear the noise, but in the serenest sky that ever I saw, being without all cloud, did to my thinking see the place from which it came. (p. 134)

Herbert, whose philosophical treatises were to be discussed by Gassendi and Descartes; who was later to be denounced, along with Spinoza and Hobbes, as a free-thinker; Herbert, who on his death-bed was refused the last Sacrament by Archbishop Ussher because of his sceptical attitude; this same Herbert invokes the sanction of the Deity for the publication of his speculations, and blandly records the miracle by which he was assured of divine approval. One can only compare him with a remarkably agile equestrian artist in a circus, leaping with nonchalance from a horse going in one direction to one headed the other way.

In his lifetime Herbert was noted for his versatility. John Donne, the devoted friend of his mother, addressed to him at the siege of Juliers a poem on the complex nature of man, concluding with the lines:

> As brave as true, is that profession than
> Which you do use to make; that you know man.
> This makes it credible; you have dwelt upon
> All worthy bookes, and now are such a one.
> Actions are authors, and of those in you
> Your friends find every day a mart of new.
>
> (Grierson ed., vol. 1, p. 195)

Herbert's own account of his activities at Juliers does not even faintly suggest that he was a man of learning or experience, but only one of reckless courage. He tells how he and Colonel Balagny, a former rival, dared one another to leave the trenches and make towards the city across a stretch of exposed ground, drawing upon themselves such a storm of enemy bullets that the Frenchman remarked, 'It is very hot here.' 'I answered briefly thus,' says Herbert:

> 'You shall go first, or else I will never go'; hereupon he ran with all speed, and somewhat crouching, towards the trenches. I followed after, leisurely and upright, and yet came within the trenches before they on the bulwark or cortine could charge again; which passage afterwards being related to the Prince of Orange, he said it was a strange bravado of Balagny, and that we went to an unavoidable death. I could relate divers things of note concerning myself, during the siege; but do forbear, lest I should relish too much of vanity. . . . (p. 62)

His best friends knew him for something far better than a popinjay. Ben Jonson, with whom he had a lifelong acquaintance and a fair amount of literary commerce, was not given to servile flattery, but he eulogised Herbert in lines that suggest that here indeed is the *uomo universale*, the complete gentleman, the type of manly perfection which Renaissance education was geared to produce.

> If men get fame for some one vertue: Then,
> What man art thou, that art so many men,
> All-vertuous Herbert! on whose every part
> *Truth* might spend all her voyce, *Fame* all her art.
> Whether thy learning they would take, or wit,
> Or valour, or thy judgment seasoning it,
> Thy standing upright to thy selfe, thy ends
> Like straight; thy pietie to God, and friends:
> Their latter praise would still the greatest bee,
> And yet, they, all together, less than thee.[1]

Aubrey, so often spiteful, does not indulge in gossip, but refers to 'the learned Lord Herbert of Cherbury', who numbered John Donne among his friends, lived at the Castle of Montgomery, 'a most romancy seat', and had prayers twice daily in his house—thus bearing out Ben Jonson's remark about 'pietie to God'. It is, however, from Aubrey that we have the story of Herbert's death-bed, when he showed no distress at being deprived of the last Sacrament; so that, again, we are faced with the contradictions of Herbert's nature and behaviour.

Perhaps a clue to these can be found in his upbringing. He lost his father when he was in his early teens and had just begun his studies at Oxford. From the *Autobiography* it is clear that Edward admired his handsome, bold and just-dealing father, and that he took a great pride in his Herbert ancestors, mainly on account of their prowess as fighters. Walton, in his *Life of George Herbert*, remarks that he came from 'a Family, that hath been blessed with men of remarkable wisdom, and a willingness to serve their Country, and indeed to do good to all Mankind; for which they are eminent . . .'.[2] The tradition of

---

[1] *Poems*, ed. B. H. Newdigate, 1936, p. 38.
[2] Walton's *Lives*, World's Classics, p. 260.

public service and of hospitality is duly stressed by Edward
Herbert, but he dwells less on their wisdom.

It is from Walton that we know far more about Edward's
mother than he himself tells in the *Autobiography*; and his
marked silences suggest that theirs was a difficult relationship.
Magdalen Herbert, the daughter of well-to-do Shropshire
landowners, the Newports, was a remarkable woman. Left a
widow at the age of thirty, with seven sons and three daughters,
the last son born after his father's death, she did not remain
among her kinsfolk on the Welsh borders but removed to
Oxford, so that her children could enjoy a good education.
Edward, already entered at University College, was soon
prudently married to a wealthy Herbert cousin, some years
older than himself. He never, in the *Autobiography*, manifests
any feeling for his wife, beyond priding himself on having
remained faithful to her for the first ten years of their marriage.
She is mentioned as providing, at Oxford, 'a due remedy for
that lasciviousness to which youth is naturally inclined'.
Young Mrs Herbert lived in the house of her mother-in-law,
and though Walton paints an idyllic picture of the relationship
between mother and son, it is more than likely that Edward
found her devotion oppressive.

Having . . . provided him a fit *Tutor*, she commended him to his
Care; yet she continued there with him, and still kept him in a
moderate awe of her self: and so much under her own eye, as to
see and converse with him daily; but she managed this power
over him without any rigid sourness, as might make her company
a torment to her Child; but with such a sweetness and complyance
with the recreations and pleasures of youth, as did incline him
willingly to spend much time in the company of his dear and
careful Mother; which was to her great content. . . . (Ibid.,
p. 264)

To her, no doubt, it was delightful, but her high-spirited

son must have often have been irked by this over-anxious supervision. There is a revealing little passage in the *Autobiography*:

> ... I cannot swim, for, as I was once in danger of drowning, by learning to swim, my mother, upon her blessing, charged me never to learn swimming, telling me further, that she had heard of more drowned than saved by it, which reason, though it did not prevail with me, yet her commandment did. (p. 41)

Perhaps the belligerency and sheer masculine vanity that so colour the *Autobiography* represent a reaction against too much feminine domination in Edward Herbert's youth. That he felt real resentment against his mother for her second marriage is certain. He does not so much as mention it, or refer, except in a trivial context, to his young step-father, Sir John Danvers. Walton and Donne write in idyllic terms about this marriage, but Edward may well have been disturbed by it, for his mother was over forty at the time and her new husband, exceptionally handsome and agreeable, was young enough to be her son. There is a rather pathetic letter, written by Lady Danvers to Edward while he was on his continental travels in 1615, which suggests an ungracious attitude on his part:

> My deare Sonne, it is straunge to me to here you to complayne of want of care of you in your absence, when my thoughts are seldom removed from you which must assuredly set me aworkynge of any thynge that may doe you good. ...

She then speaks of the love and generosity which her husband always manifests towards Edward, continuing,

> Mistake him not but beleeve me there was never a tenderer hart or a lovinger mind in any man then is in him towards you who have power to comaund him in all that is his. ... Your wife and sweet children are well, and herein I send you little Florence

letter to see what comfort you may have of your deare children. Let them, my deare Sonne, draw you home and affoorde them your care and me your comfort that desire more to see you then I desire any thinge ells in the world.[1]

Besides resentment against a young step-father, Edward seems to have been annoyed on financial grounds at his mother's remarriage. There are several indications in the *Autobiography* that he thought his mother a bad manager of money, and he goes out of his way to praise his maternal grandmother, Lady Newport, because she did not re-marry but gave the management of her estates to her eldest son.

Donne addressed several poems to Magdalen Herbert, and it was she who inspired his lovely lines:

> No Spring, nor Summer Beauty hath such grace,
> As I have seen in one Autumnall face.

(Grierson ed., vol., p. 92)

All that her eldest son can find to say about her is that she lived virtuously and lovingly with his father, brought up her children carefully, 'and, briefly, was that woman Dr Donne hath described in his funeral sermon of her printed'. It was indeed an eloquent and moving sermon; but if a son falls back on second-hand testimonials to a mother of exceptional goodness, intelligence and beauty, there is something very wrong with their relationship.

The religious atmosphere in which Edward Herbert was reared left an indelible mark on his mind. The reflections upon the soul and its relationship to God which appear in the *Autobiography* are not always specifically Christian, but they show a large charity of judgement and a deep seriousness. Against the success-story which occupies the major part of the book may be set thoughtful passages from the first section;

---

[1] *Montgomeryshire Collections XX*, (1886), pp. 85–6, quoted by Harold E. Hutcheson in *Religio Laici*, p. 11.

and one long reflection in particular provides a telling comment on the values so gaily asserted elsewhere. Faith, hope and love seem to Herbert faculties that prove man to be destined for immortality,

> ... since they never rest or fix upon any transitory or perishing object in this world, as extending themselves to something further than can be here given, and indeed acquiesce only in the perfect, eternal and infinite: I confess they are of some use here; yet I appeal to everybody, whether any worldly felicity did so satisfy their hope here, that they did not wish and hope for something more excellent, or whether they had ever that faith in their own wisdom, or in the help of man, that they were not constrained to have recourse to some diviner and superior power, than they could find on earth, to relieve them in their danger or necessity; whether ever they could place their love on any earthly beauty, that it did not fade and wither, if not frustrate and deceive them, or whether ever their joy was so consummate in anything they delighted in, that they did not want much more than it, or indeed than this world can afford, to make them happy. The proper object of these faculties, therefore, though framed, or at least appearing in this world, is God only, upon whom faith, hope, and love were never placed in vain, or remain long unrequited. (p. 19)

Besides inclining his mind to the study of religion, Mrs Herbert must also have encouraged her eldest son's interest in medicine. Donne in his funeral sermon relates that

> as her house was a court, with conversation of the best, and an almshouse in feeding the poor, so was it also a hospital in ministering relief to the sick. And truly, the love of doing good in this kind, of ministering to the sick, was the honey that spread over all her bread. . . . (*Appendix* p. 179)

Edward Herbert not only manifests a great interest in drugs and prescriptions, but he relates several cures which he actually performed. A gentleman, he thinks, should learn both the diagnostic and the prognostic parts of medicine, and how to prepare remedies with his own hands and administer them. George Herbert in *A Priest to the Temple* similarly assumes that the country parson will be able at need to act as physician to his flock, and shares with his elder brother an interest in the curative properties of herbs. 'Home-bred medicines are . . . familiar for all men's bodyes.'[1]

Edward Herbert's interest in plants extended to a genuine enthusiasm for botany. When Thomas Johnson, the learned editor of Gerard's *Herbal*, made the first serious botanic tour of Wales in 1639 he and his companions were hospitably entertained at Montgomery Castle. Herbert's domestic chaplain was one William Coote, a notable collector of plants; and in the *Autobiography* he recommends botany as a rewarding pursuit, describing how a gentleman should go hunting for various species of plants, carrying with him, or causing his servant to carry, the illustrations cut out from some good Herbal, so that he can identify his finds.

Edward Herbert, as a young man living at home, taught himself French, Italian and Spanish, with the aid of dictionaries and books of idioms; and in music he showed an aptitude that, again, he shared with his brother George. Donne in his funeral sermon makes special mention of the music-making in Mrs Herbert's household, so that it is not surprising to read in the *Autobiography*:

> I attained also to sing my part at first sight in music, and to play on the lute with very little or almost no teaching :—my intention in learning languages being to make myself a citizen of the world as far as it were possible; and my learning of music was for this end, that I might entertain myself at home, and together refresh my mind after my studies, to which I was exceedingly inclined. . . . (p. 23)

[1] *The Works of George Herbert*, ed. F. E. Hutchinson, Oxford, 1941, p. 261.

Herbert was not exaggerating his interest in things of the mind, and there are occasional indications, even in the latter part of the *Autobiography*, that he was a two-sided man; he mentions, for instance, a meeting in Paris with Isaac Casaubon, and a lecture he attended at Padua by the Aristotelian scholar Cremonini; yet, once he is launched upon the tale of his escapades, his intellectual life recedes into the distant background. It is as though he far preferred being his father's son, a fiery Welshman, handsome, intrepid, quixotically honourable, to being the son of his mother, studious, religiously inclined, the friend of poets.

He certainly seems to throw off shackles when he turns from educational themes to his own adventures in the great world. The pace quickens, his fancy comes to the aid of his memory, and a highly entertaining narrative is the result. Not all the amusement derives from the lively descriptions and dialogues; part of it comes from Herbert's unconsciousness of his own absurdity. It was this that sent Horace Walpole and Gray into such fits of laughter that, when they tried to read the manuscript aloud to comfort the disconsolate Lady Waldegrave, they 'could not get on for laughing and screaming'.[1]

With what gravity, for instance, Herbert introduces the topic of his portrait:

And now, if I may say it without vanity, I was in great esteem both in court and city: many of the greatest desiring my company, though yet before that time I had no acquaintance with them. Richard, Earl of Dorset, to whom otherwise I was a stranger, one day invited me to Dorset House, where bringing me into his gallery, and showing me many pictures, he at last brought me to a frame covered with green taffeta, and asked me who I thought was there; and therewithal presently drawing the curtain, showed

[1] Letter to Montagu, 16/vii/1764 (Walpole's *Letters*, ed. Cunningham, vol. ii, p. 252).

me my own picture; whereupon demanding how his Lordship came to have it, he answered, that he had heard so many brave things of me, that he got a copy of a picture which one Larkin a painter drew for me. . . . (p. 68)

Herbert then relates how someone much greater, whom he dares not name (presumably Queen Anne, whose marked favours he mentions elsewhere), also had a copy made and placed it, quite without his knowledge, in her cabinet, which caused great gossip after her death. Then, with obvious relish, he tells at length the story of Lady Ayres, one of the queen's waiting-women, who had a miniature copy made of this same portrait, which she caused to be set in gold and enamel,

> and so wore it about her neck so low that she hid it under her breasts, which I conceive coming afterwards to the knowledge of Sir John Ayres, gave him more cause for jealousy than needed, had he known how innocent I was from pretending to anything which might wrong him or his lady; since I could not so much as imagine that either she had my picture, or that she bare more than ordinary affection to me. . . . (p. 69)

So far, so good; but Herbert's vanity gets the better of his discretion, and he cannot resist adding a sequel which rather spoils the effect of his protestations of innocence and in-difference:

> Coming one day into her chamber, I saw her through the curtains lying upon her bed with a wax candle in one hand, and the picture I formerly mentioned in the other. I coming there-upon somewhat boldly to her, she blew out the candle, and hid the picture from me; myself thereupon being curious to know what it was she held in her hand, got the candle to be lighted again, by means whereof I found it was my picture she looked upon with more earnestness and passion than I could have easily believed, especially since myself was not engaged in any affection towards her: I could willingly have omitted this passage, but that

it was the beginning of a bloody history which followed. . . .
(p. 69)

—a duel with the not unnaturally jealous husband.

Herbert had a passion for duelling which persisted even
after he had been made an ambassador and was a public
personage. More often than not these affairs, provoked by the
slightest of fancied affronts, petered out harmlessly. Better
evidence of his courage is provided by the story of how he
attacked, single-handed, a gang of thieves who came to his
house to rob him of the gold he had just received as travelling
expenses for his Paris mission. His servants were lodged elsewhere, so

> As soon as I heard the noise, I suspected presently they came to rob
> me of my money; however, I thought fit to rise, and go to the
> window to know where they were; the first word I heard was:
> 'Darest thou come down, Welshman?' which I no sooner heard,
> but, taking a sword in one hand, and a little target in the other, I
> did in my shirt run down the stairs, open the doors suddenly,
> and charged ten or twelve of them with that fury that they ran
> away, some throwing away their halberts, others hurting their
> fellows to make them go faster in a narrow way they were to
> pass; in which disordered manner I drove them to the middle of
> the street by the Exchange, where finding my bare feet hurt by
> the stones I trod on, I thought fit to return home, and leave them
> to their flight. (p. 99)

Every autobiographer must be swayed by two contrary
tendencies—the wish to assert himself and the wish not to
give himself away. In Herbert they seem to have operated very
oddly. He suppresses what, as a philosopher, he should surely
have regarded as the more valuable side of his life, his intellectual
and literary undertakings, and delights in recalling and embel-
lishing all sorts of manly exploits in which he does not always
cut quite the dash that he imagines. No doubt the active life

was more amusing and easy to write about than the life of the mind, which perhaps he considered was sufficiently expressed in the treatises and poems that he had left for posterity; and it must, moreover, be remembered, when the *Autobiography* is criticised as an unbalanced book, that it is incomplete.

It breaks off at the very point when Herbert's successful public life came to a sudden end. In 1624 James I sent two Ambassadors Extraordinary to Paris, to negotiate the marriage between Prince Charles and Henrietta Maria. Herbert was already engaged on these negotiations, but was conducting them with a political frankness that annoyed both the French and his own sovereign. In the summer of 1624 he was recalled to England, and thereafter hoped and pleaded in vain for further employment in the service of the state. He was deeply in debt, and the Treasury owed him arrears of salary. He had influential friends, but all that he received from James I in the way of reward for five years of faithful service in Paris was an Irish barony. In 1629 he was given the title of Baron Herbert of Cherbury in the English peerage, but he was fobbed off with minor offices, unworthy of his capacities. By the time that he began to write his autobiography, at the age of sixty, he knew that his sun of public success had set twenty years earlier. Nostalgia for happier days may have a good deal to do with Herbert's treatment of his life story.

The twenty unrecorded years included a great amount of private study, for Herbert's mental resources were too powerful to permit him merely to waste his time. In order to ingratiate himself with Charles I, he turned historian; but neither his account of Buckingham's ill-fated expedition to the Island of Rhé nor his *Life of Henry VIII* brought him the royal recognition that he had desired. Although his account of Henry VIII is eulogistic, the book shows that Herbert had a sound understanding of what is required of a serious biographer. He was assigned rooms at Whitehall in which to prosecute his researches in State papers, and he enlisted the help of Thomas Master, a Fellow of New College, in going through a mass of historical documents from various sources. Bacon's *Life of Henry VII* was his inspiration, but his own book is no masterpiece; it lacks the stylistic vitality of the *Autobiography*, and is a ponderous compilation. 'In the intervals of history', Miss Wedgwood notes, 'he solicited the King's attention for various practical inventions of his own—gun-carriages, naval equipment, and a floating bathing establishment to be installed on the Thames.'[1]

By far the most important achievements of his leisure years were his Latin works, *Religio Laici* and *De Religione Gentilium*. The former was published in 1645 together with an appendix to *De Veritate* entitled *De Causis Errorum*; the latter did not appear until 1663 in an edition published in Amsterdam. The nature of truth and the essentials of religious belief were topics that had interested Herbert throughout his life and they were the themes that most profitably occupied his mind during his years of retirement.

The pressure of a very devout and orthodox Anglican upbringing may have originally touched off in Edward Herbert the impulse to question the very fundamentals of religion. In his travels abroad, and especially during his residence in France, he had had plenty of opportunity to observe the results—and, indeed, the practice—of religious persecution. He remarked that zealous and intolerant proselytisers were often disputing and coercing about inessentials, and came to the conclusion that humanity would be behaving more rationally if it could agree upon a corpus of fundamental religious notions; and such notions, he believed, could be discovered in existent religions and in the beliefs of antiquity.

[1] *The King's Peace*, 1955, pp. 68-9.

These principles of natural religion he formulated at the end of
De Veritate. This book for the most part is strictly philosophical,
and in it Herbert attempts to work out a theory of knowledge
and to analyse the criteria by which men recognise truth; but
it was his formulation of a Deistic creed that made his name
famous. The common consent of mankind, he asserted, would
be given to the propositions that there is a supreme and
providential Deity, who must be worshipped, and who can
best be worshipped not by ceremonies but by virtuous living;
also that men must in this life repent and expiate their wrong-
doings, and that they can look forward to reward or punish-
ment after death. All specific religious cults, in Herbert's
opinion, were derived from these archetypal notions, and in his
two later books he foreshadowed the study of comparative
religions in his attempt to find grounds on which a universal
religious toleration might be built. This dispassionate curiosity
he combined with a good deal of speculative energy; yet he
duly observed the requirements of the established religion of
his own country, and indeed had a lively faith in the special
intervention of Providence in the affairs of his daily life.

It is conceivable that if Herbert had continued his *Autobiography* he might have redressed its unevenness by some
account of his intellectual activities during his later years; but
it is pretty clear that the old man lost heart when he came to the
point in his life-story at which his grandeur was eclipsed. His
withdrawal from Paris had meant the end of his public career;
and when he took up his pen nearly twenty years later, we
know that he was a tired and disheartened man. Writing in
1643 to his brother Sir Henry Herbert, Master of the Revels,
he remarks, 'I find myself older in this one year than in fifty-
nine years before'; and it was just then that he embarked upon
his autobiography.

The Civil War had broken out, and Herbert was unwillingly involved in it. His son Richard had raised a troop of horse for Prince Rupert in 1642 and had joined the Royalist forces in Shrewsbury; but Lord Herbert, though he had gone on a Royalist expedition to Scotland in 1639, refused to associate himself openly with Prince Rupert. In 1644 he made terms with the Parliamentary troops who were threatening Montgomery Castle, in order to preserve his library and to secure his personal safety. His Royalist neighbours, outraged at his treachery, laid siege to the castle, and Herbert departed to London, under the protection of the Parliamentarians. There he devoted himself to literary work, corresponding with foreign scholars and visiting Gassendi in Paris. In his will, made in 1648, he made generous provision for his descendants, which suggests that the political differences between them were, on his part, a matter for regret. His Greek and Latin books that were with him in London he left to Jesus College, Oxford, 'for the inception of a library there', and he directed that his *Autobiography* should be completed by 'a person whom I shall by word entreat'. He died in 1648 and was buried in the church of St Giles in the Fields. Although he desired a monument to be set up in Montgomery Church, this was not done, and the Castle, that 'romancy seat', was destroyed in 1649.

The completion of the *Autobiography* was never accomplished, and the manuscript remained half forgotten among the Powis family archives until Horace Walpole in 1764 published it at Strawberry Hill. In his dedication to the owner of the original, Walpole remarks, 'Hitherto Lord Herbert has been little known as an author. I much mistake if hereafter he is not considered as one of the most extraordinary characters which this country has produced.' He had experienced considerable difficulty in getting Lord Powis to allow the publication of the memoirs, because of their oddity, but succeeded in flattering him into giving his consent, with the result that after a few months he could write to Montagu, 'The thing most in fashion is my edition of Lord Herbert's Life: people are mad after it . . .' (*Letters*, p. 302)

Laughter-provoking the book may be, yet it is an original, serious and valuable attempt at an autobiography by a man who was, even by the standards of his contemporaries, extraordinary indeed. To Walpole and his friends the combination of Don Quixote, Don Juan and moral philosopher must have seemed even more comic and incongruous than it does to our generation, which is accustomed to think of the seventeenth century as a period that fostered complex characters.

Edward Herbert matured at a time when the Renaissance ideal of the *uomo universale* had not yet given way to the modern conception of the expert and specialist. For all his vanity and lack of humour, he is a late but fine specimen of the *cortegiano*. He conscientiously cultivated all the accomplishments of mind and body that would fit him for the society of princes and enable him to play his part as a gentleman in the service of his country. Typically, he understressed the depth and breadth of his intellectual interests. A Renaissance gentleman was expected to wear his learning lightly. And, indeed, as a philosopher he was essentially an amateur, with that independence of mind which is too often denied to the professional student of systems of thought.

But can we leave it at that? Does the *Autobiography* leave us with the impression of an integrated man, who had successfully fused the active and contemplative strains in his own nature? Surely not. There is such a discrepancy of tone and attitude between the reflective and the adventurous portions of the book that we are led to suspect an unresolved conflict between 'the learned Lord Herbert' and the successful worldling whom he portrays with such enjoyment. The strange omissions, the disingenuous distortions, the protestations of veracity and the high moral pretensions, together with the self-flattery and frivolity; these do not suggest a man at peace with himself and sure of his values.

For years his brother George was torn between the contrary impulses of his nature, which in his case objectified themselves as the counter-attractions of Court and Church. Eventually he made the costly decision to surrender his worldly ambitions, and achieved the blessing of complete singleness of mind and heart and will. Edward Herbert's life was one of compromise. He was gifted with a remarkable intellect and striking good looks, besides plenty of effrontery and powerful friends. The very abundance of his potentialities was his undoing. Though he enjoyed a few years of success, his public achievements did not really amount to much; and he seems to have derived little personal satisfaction from the private life of study which, after all, secured him his fame. His final treachery to his Royalist family and neighbours for the sake of peace and quiet is a sad comment on the chivalrous ideals so loudly proclaimed in the *Autobiography*.

Lord Herbert of Cherbury, when he began the chronicle of his life, must have already suspected that he was a failure. It was too hard an admission for a proud man to make. The *Autobiography* is his brave attempt to disguise this sense of failure from himself and his posterity by recording other, more heartening, facts. If the book does not ring wholly true, if we often ask ourselves, which is the man and which the mask, the reason is that Herbert, so concerned with the nature and pursuit of *Veritas*, was not scrupulously honest with himself.

Bunyan's 'Grace Abounding'

❧

The man who sets out to recount the dealings with God with his soul is attempting something well beyond the range of the chronicler of historically verifiable circumstance and event; and he treads an even more hazardous path than he who recalls his past in order to understand his present self.

The truth of any autobiography is bound to be personal and subjective to some degree, and it is especially difficult for men or women concerned with the interior drama of conversion or spiritual pilgrimage to write in a balanced and dispassionate way. Their theme is bound to have, for themselves, an intense emotional value of a kind that is perilously difficult to communicate. Not only this; their attention will be given to mundane events and to human beings only in so far as these can clearly be seen to have affected the all-important inner life. Moreover, they survey their past as if from some high vantage-ground. The region of error, through which they have made their painful way, is not so distant that they cannot recognise its landmarks; but these are seen from an altitude, and consequently not quite as they appeared when they were originally encountered.

The ambiguity of the word Confession gives a clue to the dangers and difficulties that this type of autobiographer is bound to meet. A confession may be the acknowledgment of one's sins or the avowal of one's faith. It may also be the disclosure of matters that might have been kept secret, as prejudicial to oneself—a sense demonstrated by Rousseau, whose

Confessions have no religious purpose, but are simply self-revealing. But the *Confessions* of St Augustine are simultaneously an act of worship and an act of penance. He confesses the mercy of God in saving him, he confesses his long resistance to God's grace. The complexity of his undertaking goes beyond this, for the book takes the form of a colloquy with God. Augustine was quite aware of the equivocal nature of his enterprise: a motion of the heart, he admits, is sufficient to express contrition or praise; there is no necessity to tell the Omniscient the story of his life, far less to write down and make public his self-searchings and his prayers. He therefore admits another motive—that of influencing his fellow-men. He is suspicious of the purity of his own intentions and of the profit that his writings may afford to others; yet he believes that his brethren may rejoice at his testimony and pray for him.

> What therefore have I to do with men, that they should hear my confessions, as if it were they that would cure all that is evil in me? Men are a race curious to know of other men's lives, but slothful to correct their own. Why should they wish to hear from me what I am, when they do not wish to hear from You what they are themselves? . . . I, O Lord, confess to You that men may hear. . . . To such then as You command me to serve will I show, not what I was, but what I am now, what I continue to be. But I do not judge myself. . . .[1]

Augustine acknowledges yet another motive, though he only mentions it in passing; the confession of past sins, he says, awakens his heart from lethargy. To a man so passionately concerned with his own psychology, the recollection and expression of inner conflicts must have been an immense relief, a pleasurable and healing activity. This cathartic impulse is always present, though often not acknowledged, in the confessional type of autobiography. After all, it is the need to

[1] *The Confessions of St Augustine*, tr. F. J. Sheed, 1945, pp. 167–9.

unburden themselves that brings many people to auricular confession; the actual putting into words of obscure feelings of guilt and misery affords a measure of relief.

Augustine's foremost, conscious, concern is to glorify God. In his longing to know God, he desires to arrive at the truth about himself, and this involves him in an account of his conversion which is at once penitential and praise-giving in its intention. His second conscious purpose is to impart his experience of regeneration to his fellows; pride and humility, one suspects, are both at work here. And the third, almost unacknowledged but probably very powerful factor that drove him to write the *Confessions* was the need to relieve his own heart and clarify his own mind.

These three elements of devotion, propaganda and catharsis are present in varying degrees in all 'spiritual' autobiographies. In those of the great saints, like Augustine or Teresa of Avila, whose vision is focused on the Divine, the prayerful element predominates. Here we have scrupulous sincerity, and a moral sensibility that makes their confessions trustworthy. In lesser people, the desire to edify the brethren is likely to be dominant, and here the reader must be wary, since propagandists have their own criteria of values, and self-advertisement tends to creep in under the guise of humility.

The spiritual and intellectual grandeur of St Augustine puts his *Confessions* among the greatest and most original books in the world, and to mention John Bunyan and his *Grace Abounding* in the same breath may seem rather ridiculous; yet the great book does illuminate the small one, if only in the matter of the three mixed motives. They are all there in Bunyan, but in a different order of importance. The book is not devotional in form; there is a very evident wish to praise God by a recital of His particular mercies, but this is subordinated to the declared object of edification. Of the cathartic motive he says nothing—possibly it was unconscious; yet no reader can miss the compulsion that urged Bunyan to rid himself here of haunting memories.

Grace Abounding to the Chief of Sinners is the most poignantly personal of all the autobiographical studies produced in seventeenth-century England; yet its very title, emotionally extravagant as it is, provokes the question, how far is it trustworthy as a record of experience? The diction, the rhythms, the imagery are so forceful, the torments and ecstasies described so peculiar, that they give the immediate impression of burning sincerity; nor would an honest and godly man like Bunyan wilfully have falsified a syllable. In his Preface he writes:

> I could also have stepped into a style much higher than this in which I have now discoursed, and could have adorned all things more than I here have seemed to do, but I dare not. God did not play in convincing of me, the devil did not play in tempting of me, neither did I play when I sunk as into a bottomless pit, when the pangs of hell caught hold upon me; wherefore I may not play in my relating of them, but be plain and simple, and lay down the thing as it was.[1]

It is the declaration of a conscientious man, one who is writing 'as ever in his great Task-master's eye'; and yet the question of autobiographical reliability inevitably arises, because the religious propagandist selects and interprets the events of his life according to a scale of values very different from those of the secular historian.

Grace Abounding is a conversion-narrative, one of the many that were written in the latter half of the seventeenth century by sectarians of various persuasions. Itinerant preachers, especially if they were men of humble origin and trade, were

---

[1] *Grace Abounding*, Everyman Edition, p. 5. Subsequent page references are to this edition.

particularly given to writing down, for the edification of their
brethren, the tale of how they had been snatched as brands
from the burning and called to the ministry of the word. Their
spiritual ascendancy depended on no vocational training or
formal ordination, but simply on their own conviction of a
special calling. Their gifts in evangelism were their prime
means of persuading others that they had been singled out by
the Holy Spirit. However, a circumstantial account of his
conversion and election would naturally lend authority to the
claims of an uneducated layman to be a God-given leader, and
these narratives multiplied. Bunyan the Baptist tinker had a
rival in Benjamin Keach the Baptist tailor, also a prolific
writer of allegories and pious pamphlets, and there were
innumerable lay preachers among the Quakers and Ranters
and other socially discredited sects who earned their livings, as
the Apostles had done before them, in plying their 'mechanick'
trades. Mr York Tindall[1] claims to have read no fewer than
two thousand tracts by seventeenth-century lay-preachers,
their friends and enemies, and he has succeeded in proving with
a wealth of evidence that *Grace Abounding* belongs to an
accepted *genre*, that its emotional tone is common to many
conversion narratives, and that even the sequence of spiritual
development follows a more or less conventional pattern; but
though the surfeit of edifying pamphlets seems to have made
him impatient and contemptuous of the whole enthusiastic
crew, he cannot undermine the essential integrity of Bunyan's
story.

Grace Abounding, written during Bunyan's imprisonment in
Bedford gaol, was published in 1666. The spiritual struggles
which it recounts were a dozen years and more behind him,
and in the preface he assumes the tone of a father-in-God

[1] *John Bunyan: Mechanick Preacher*, William York Tindall, Columbia U.P.,
1934.

addressing his children. His imprisonment had set the seal of martyrdom on his already excellent reputation as preacher and pamphleteer. His motive, then, was not to recommend himself so much as to strengthen and edify his adherents by an account of the progress of his soul under the mercy of God. Though it often gives the impression that Bunyan is pouring out his pent-up troubles for the first time, without premeditation, the book is actually the fruit of long reflection—emotion recollected in tranquillity; and this again provokes the question, how far is it trustworthy as a record of experience? How far has Bunyan arranged his material and heightened his effects, in his 'Brief Relation of the Exceeding Mercy of Christ to his poor servant'?

Professor Henri Talon, in his sympathetic and learned study of Bunyan, has examined *Grace Abounding* with just these questions in mind.[1] He acquits Bunyan of any wilful distortion of fact, but reminds us that his metaphysics falsified his psychology. His retrospective vision was coloured by his later piety, and to some extent by the fashion for highly-pitched conversion narratives. Bunyan interprets as providential and miraculous happenings which at the time may have seemed no more than lucky; he exaggerates his own youthful depravity in order to show the magnitude of the change that God's abounding grace has wrought in him, and perhaps from a more self-regarding motive exaggerates the poverty and low estate of his parents. Moreover, he revised *Grace Abounding* with the conscious aim of increasing its didactic value. Professor Talon points to a number of passages, some of them very striking and significant, which were inserted in the third edition of the book. Although at first sight *Grace Abounding* appears ingenuous—for Bunyan was an intensely emotional

[1] *John Bunyan—the Man and his Works*, tr. Barbara Wall, 1951 (Paris ed. 1948).

man, with a mind unsophisticated by secular learning—Talon stresses the fact that it is in its way a work of art.

What differentiates this book from the conversion stories of worthy Quakers and other sectarians of the seventeenth century is Bunyan's superior power of conveying the momentousness of his experiences. All these converts claim to have endured paroxysms of remorse, doubt and despair and to have received personal assurance of salvation. Nor is there any reason to accuse them of hypocrisy. The religious climate of the time was full of electric storms and encouraged the display of individual disturbances. Besides, as William James wisely and charitably observed, 'A small man's salvation will always be a great salvation and the greatest of all facts *for him*.'[1] But Bunyan's imaginative powers and his command of the English language set him far above the rank and file. He could re-live in imagination the turmoils of his youth and could also find terms to describe them which, by their sheer nervous strength and intensity, convince us of the authenticity of his experiences.

In proof of this may be cited the paragraphs about the fascination which bell-ringing had for him as a young man; a vivid, obsessional story which did not appear in the first editions of *Grace Abounding*.

Now, you must know, that before this I had taken much delight in ringing, but my conscience beginning to be tender, I thought such practice was but vain, and therefore forced myself to leave it, yet my mind hankered; wherefore I should go to the steeple-house and look on it, though I durst not ring. But I thought this did not become religion neither, yet I forced myself, and would look on still; but quickly after, I began to think, How, if one of the bells should fall? Then I chose to stand under a main beam, that lay overthwart the steeple, from side to side, thinking there I might stand sure, but then I should think again, should the bell fall with a swing, it might first hit the wall, and then rebounding

[1] *Varieties of Religious Experience*, 1939 ed., p. 239.

upon me, might kill me for all this beam. This made me stand
in the steeple door; and now, thought I, I am safe enough; for,
if a bell should then fall, I can slip out behind these thick walls,
and so be preserved notwithstanding.

So, after this, I would yet go to see them ring, but would not
go farther than the steeple door; but then it came into my head,
How, if the steeple itself should fall? And this thought, it may
fall for aught I know, when I stood and looked on, did continually
so shake my mind that I durst not stand at the steeple door any
longer, but was forced to flee, for fear the steeple should fall on
my head. (p. 15)

This story seems to have been an afterthought, inserted in order
to impress upon his brethren the distance he had progressed
since his unregenerate days; but fictitious it cannot be. Only
someone who had lived through these episodes in all their
abnormality could recall them in such circumstantial phrases.
Like Rousseau, Bunyan may be arbitrary or forgetful about
facts, but he cannot go wrong about what he has felt, or about
what his feelings have led him to do.

Bunyan's adherence to truth was not literal-minded or
all-inclusive. The very sincerity of his wish to encourage the
faithful made him over-dramatise his own emotional conflicts,
and his desire to glorify God made him minimise the importance of human agents in his conversion and leave unsaid very
much that would appear vitally important to a more mundane
kind of biographer. He does not, for instance, mention the
names of his father or mother—the Bedford congregation
might be assumed to know them, as they would certainly know
that Elstow was his birthplace, though he does not name or
describe the village in his narrative. But Bunyan would have
echoed St Augustine's dictum that life does not begin with
father and mother but with God and Sin.

Grace Abounding is a recapitulation of the long quest for
salvation that culminated in Bunyan's conviction that he was

one of the elect. The greater part of the narrative is devoted to the tribulations which he underwent while he was still uncertain whether he was saved or damned. He was only twenty-five when he was baptised in the Ouse by the Baptist minister Gifford—an event which, oddly enough, is not alluded to in his story—so that it is a young man's spiritual autobiography written down after years of stability.

The book consists of a preface, written in a Pauline epistolary vein, and strongly interlaced with scriptural quotations; a long account of Bunyan's spiritual struggles from boyhood until the time when he at last felt the conviction of personal salvation; and a brief account of his call to the ministry of preaching, and of his imprisonment. Modern editions of *Grace Abounding* supplement it with the further *Relation of my Imprisonment*, a most vivid story, partly in dialogue, which was handed down in manuscript in Bunyan's family, to be printed first in 1765. It provides an excellent conclusion to the conversion-narrative, if only because it testifies to the real change that a certitude of personal salvation wrought in John Bunyan's character. The morbidly sensitive man wrestling with obsessions has been converted into a steadfast, not to say pertinacious, spokesman for the liberty of dissenters. The process of release from tormenting doubts and fears had been slow, full of setbacks, anything but steady; but when the time came for Bunyan to confront external dangers and difficulties, he had acquired unshakeable confidence. He met the hostility of magistrates, trial and imprisonment with the most exemplary fortitude. His conversion stands the pragmatic test of Jonathan Edwards, the famous New England Puritan: 'The degree in which our experience is productive of practice shows the degree in which our experience is spiritual and divine.'

Bunyan's purpose was not to trace his life-history but to give an account of the dealings of God with his soul, yet the biographical interest of *Grace Abounding* is considerable, and all who have written about the man John Bunyan have drawn heavily upon it. Indeed, his purely human reminiscences are so natural and telling that the reader wishes there were more of them.

The story begins with a brief allusion to the mean and despised condition of his parents. His father was indeed a tinker, but no mere vagrant, for he owned the cottage in Elstow where young John grew up. The Bunyans conformed to the Church of England, but there is no indication that they were pious. However, they sent their son to school, where he learned to read and write. In spite of his insistence on his childish depravity, he was probably no worse than other little Bedfordshire boys, though it is to be hoped that he was exceptional in his subjection to fearful dreams and night terrors. Like other village boys, he took part in the dancing and football and rounders on the green, and went on with these pastimes when he had outgrown boyhood. When he was sixteen his mother died and his father almost at once married again. Bunyan does not mention this, but he briefly alludes to his spell of service in the same year with the Parliamentary forces. He was mustered and sent to the garrison at Newport Pagnell; but all that he records of this experience is a miraculous escape that he had when one of his companions, by his own wish, took Bunyan's place on a dangerous expedition, was shot through the head and died.

His three years with the Parliamentary army must actually have had a great influence on his intellectual and spiritual development. For the first time in his life, and at an impressionable age, he was on his own, away from the village where he had been reared, in close association with men whose religious and political convictions were antagonistic to the established order. Sir Samuel Luke, the commander of the garrison, was so prominent a Puritan that Butler took him as the model for his Hudibras. Bunyan, however, does not refer to him or to the many discussions that he must have overheard and taken part in, concerning doctrine and discipline.

He returned to Elstow without having engaged in a campaign, and presently married, while still under twenty :

> . . . and my mercy was to light upon a wife whose father was counted godly. This woman and I, though we came together as poor as might be, having not so much household stuff as a dish or spoon between us, yet this she had for her part, *The Plain Man's Pathway to Heaven*,[1] and *The Practice of Piety*,[2] which her father had left her when he died. (p. 10)

Who Bunyan's father-in-law was we do not know, beyond that he was a good Puritan who lived a strict and holy life in word and deed and 'would often reprove and correct vice, both in his house and among the neighbours'. Under the influence of his daughter, and as a result of pondering over her two treasured books, Bunyan became a reformed character. Hitherto he seems to have been a careless, rather boisterous young man, given to swearing and sport, but now he began to go to church twice a day and to feel a superstitious admiration for all that pertained to the priestly office.

From his later vantage point as a Baptist minister, Bunyan regarded this phase of his religious development as a merely superficial improvement, for he had not yet been stricken by a sense of sin, nor had he fully realised the personal implications of the awful questions dealt with by Arthur Dent in his book. Soon, however, the problem of predestination was thrust

---

[1] *The Plaine-Mans Path-Way to Heaven Wherein Every Man may Clearly see Whether he shall be Saved or Damned*, by Arthur Dent, preacher of the Word of God at South-Shoobury in Essex (1601).

[2] *The Practice of Piety directing a Christian how to walk that he may please God*, by Lewis Bayly, Bishop of Bangor (1613).

upon him, for while he was in the middle of a game of tip-cat
one Sunday after church,

> a voice did suddenly dart from heaven into my soul, which said,
> Wilt thou leave thy sins and go to heaven, or have thy sins and
> go to hell? At this I was put to an exceeding maze; wherefore,
> leaving my cat upon the ground, I looked up to heaven, and
> was, as if I had, with the eyes of my understanding, seen the
> Lord Jesus looking down upon me, as being very hotly displeased
> with me, and as if he did severely threaten me with some grievous
> punishment for these and other my ungodly practices. (p. 12)

Bunyan had already been warned in sermons by the vicar of
Elstow about the impropriety of Sunday games, and with a
nervous melancholy that was typical of him at this stage of his
life, he leapt to the conclusion that it was already too late for
him to look for pardon from Christ:

> . . . and fearing lest it should be so, I felt my heart sink in despair,
> concluding it was too late; and therefore I resolved in my mind
> I would go on in sin; for, thought I, if the case be thus, my state
> is surely miserable; miserable if I leave my sins, and but miserable
> if I follow them; I can but be damned, and if I must be so, I had
> as good be damned for many sins, as damned for few.
>
> Thus stood I in the midst of my play, before all that were
> present; but yet I told them nothing; but I say, I having made
> this conclusion, I returned desperately to my sport again. (p. 12)

By degrees, however, in spite of his occasional fits of
despairing recklessness, Bunyan gave up his games and his old
habit of swearing, and, after an immense effort, the vain
practice of bell-ringing.

He read his Bible and tried to follow the commandments,
'and, as I thought, did keep them pretty well sometimes', so
that there were occasions when 'I thought I pleased God as well
as any man in England'. The neighbours remarked on the
'great and famous reformation' in his life and manners, and

their commendations pleased him mightily. Looking back in after years from Bedford prison, he sees himself as a 'poor painted hypocrite', that 'knew not Christ, nor grace, nor faith, nor hope'; but to an impartial reader at a distance of nearly three centuries, it looks as though this moral reformation had been sound and lasting, and that very much of the credit for Bunyan's progress in religion belongs, under God, to his first wife.

By his own reckoning, however, his spiritual rebirth began on the day when he was plying his tinker's trade in Bedford and chanced to come on 'three or four poor women sitting at a door in the sun and talking about the things of God'. Bunyan, by this time himself 'a brisk talker' in matters of religion, was put to shame and shaken by the happy and confident way in which these simple women spoke of their spiritual experiences, as though they had found a new world. He began to frequent the open-communion Baptist Meeting at Bedford, and to torment himself with Calvinistic questions; had he faith? how could he recognise faith in himself? what was the new birth and could he hope to experience it? was he one of the elect? had he turned too late to the light? He was 'all on a flame' to be converted, and those who had undergone conversion seemed lovely and shining in his eyes. He was introduced to John Gifford, the pastor of the Bedford Meeting, who invited him to his house to hear others testifying. This contact with the saved seems only to have deepened Bunyan's sense of his own sinfulness, and he went through a terrible period of depression and doubt. Like a good Baptist, Gifford must have urged him to scrutinise himself for signs of election, and the constant introspection drive Bunyan almost to despair.

And now was I sorry that God made me a man, for I feared I was a reprobate; I counted man as unconverted, the most doleful of all the creatures. Thus being afflicted, and tossed about in my sad condition, I counted myself alone, and above the most of men unblessed. (p. 29)

For about a year he was storm-tossed, tempted to blasphemy, to the sin against the Holy Ghost, and to utter discouragement. 'The ministry of holy Mr Gifford' was, Bunyan says, a help to his stability, but it seems chiefly to have consisted in urging him to take no truth upon trust, but to wait for personal conviction from the Holy Spirit speaking through the scriptures. Sometimes a comforting verse from the Bible would encourage Bunyan, but its effects could be cancelled by a threatening one, and for months at a time he seems to have been at the mercy of conflicting texts that assailed him like hallucinatory voices. The scriptures 'tear and rend' his soul, or, on happier days, they 'spangle' in his eyes. A text can so haunt him that

> it would cry aloud with a very great voice 'Return unto me, for I have redeemed thee.' Indeed, this would make me a little stop, and, as it were, look over my shoulder behind me, to see if I could discern that the God of grace did follow me with a pardon in his hand, but I could no sooner do that, but all would be clouded and darkened again by that sentence, 'For you know that afterward, when he would have inherited a blessing, he found no place of repentance, though he sought it carefully with tears.' Wherefore I could not return, but fled, though at sometimes it cried, 'Return, Return,' as it did holloa after me. (p. 52)

It was after a prolonged period of consolation that he fell into the most wretched of his states, when he was tormented by an obsessive temptation to repeat the sin of Judas:

> Sometimes it would run in my thoughts, not so little as a hundred times together, Sell him, sell him, sell him; against which, I may say, for whole hours together, I have been forced to stand as continually leaning and forcing my spirit against it, lest haply, before I were aware, some wicked thought might arise in my

heart that might consent thereto. . . . This temptation did put me to such scares . . . that by the very force of my mind, in labouring to gainsay and resist this wickedness, my very body also would be put in action or motion by way of pushing or thrusting with my hands or elbows, still answering as fast as the destroyer said Sell him; I will not, I will not, I will not; no, not for thousands, thousands, thousands of worlds. (p. 43)

Small wonder that eventually, worn down, he despairingly exclaimed, 'Let him go, if he will!' And now he was convinced that he was indeed a second Judas who had sold his Master, and was irrevocably damned.

The tortures that he suffered are vividly described, with physical imagery or with reference to bodily pains that accompanied his mental anguish; but by very slow degrees he began to feel the curse lightening. One notable step out of this slough of despond was a supernatural experience which he recounts in an unusually guarded and diffident tone; he seems almost loath to impart it because of its preciousness, and thus he convinces us of its authenticity. He was walking to and fro in a good man's shop one day, in the deepest dejection, when a wind seemed to rush in at the window, and a voice asked him 'Didst thou ever refuse to be justified by the blood of Christ?' His heart answered 'groaningly', No.

Then fell with power that word of God upon me, 'See that ye refuse not him that speaketh.' This made a strange seizure on my spirit; it brought light with it, and commanded a silence in my heart of all those tumultuous thoughts that before did use, like masterless hell-hounds, to roar and bellow, and make a hideous noise within me. . . . Yea, this was a kind of chide to my proneness to desperation. . . . But as to my determining about this strange dispensation, what it was I knew not; or from whence it came I know not. I have not yet, in twenty years' time, been able to make a judgment of it. I thought then what I here shall be loath to speak. But verily, that sudden rushing wind was as if an angel had come upon me; but both it and the salvation I will leave until the day of judgement; only this I say, it commanded a great calm in my soul, it persuaded me that there might be hope. (p. 53)

Evidently Bunyan felt that this experience belonged to a different category from his constant hallucinatory voices, and relates it only because 'I am here unfolding of my secret things', and 'I thought it might not be altogether inexpedient to let this also show itself.' Certainly it was a memorable step towards the conviction of pardon and redemption. There were renewed periods of depression, but at last promises of election began to sound in his ears; he had a vision of Christ in glory, and went home rejoicing; and from that time onward he possessed the assurance, hard-won indeed, of his own salvation.

The second part of Bunyan's story, which tells of his call to the Baptist ministry of preaching, is far less vivid than the recapitulation of his inner agonies and hopes during the conversion period; but it is significant that he tells how his calls to repentance were particularly heartfelt, for 'I preached what I felt, what I smartingly did feel'. His own spiritual progress had made him acutely sensitive to the apostle Paul's warning, 'Let him that thinketh he standeth take heed lest he fall'. Conversion had been, for Bunyan, no sudden blinding illumination, but a difficult, wearying, long-drawn-out process. It had followed the lines of the classical Puritan conversion, in its three stages of conviction of sin, evangelical revelation and the final personal call of Christ; but Christian's troubles were not ended when the pack fell from his shoulders at the foot of the cross, nor need we suppose that Bunyan's distrustful, melancholic nature was instantly transformed when he received baptism at the hands of John Gifford in 1653.

He became an active lay-preacher in and around Bedford, feeling himself bound to awaken men to a sense of their fearful predicament; for though the salvation of sinners depended wholly on the free grace of God, that grace could operate more easily in troubled hearts. He moved to Bedford from Elstow in 1655, and in the following year published the first of his pamphlets, *Some Gospel Truths Opened*, which was aimed against the Quakers, the great rivals of the Baptists for the allegiance of the common people. For the next few years Bunyan combined his trade with pastoral work and preaching and religious pamphleteering; but in 1660 an end came to the freedom which the sectarians had enjoyed under the Protectorate. In December of that year Bunyan was arrested for preaching to a handful of people in 'a conventicle'. He could have avoided arrest, as he was warned of its likelihood, but he braved the authorities, refused to promise to abandon his public preaching, and was sent to Bedford Gaol.

From the very full account which Bunyan left of his trial, it is clear that he could have got off much more lightly if he had been less intransigent. The magistrates were not ill-disposed, and when he had been three months in prison the clerk of the justices tried to persuade him to be a little more accommodating; but Bunyan was ready for martyrdom. His apprehensive nature had apparently made him imagine that his imprisonment might actually end with the gallows:

> I was also at this time so really possessed with the thought of death, that oft I was as if I was on the ladder with a rope about my neck; only this was some encouragement to me, I thought I might now have an opportunity to speak my last words to a multitude, which I thought would come to see me die; and, thought I, if it must be so, if God will but convert one soul by my very last words, I shall not count my life thrown away, nor lost. (p. 100)

If this seems histrionic, we may recall John Lilburne the Leveller, who when he had been flogged and dragged through the streets of London did speak with immense effect to the citizens who were watching his sufferings. And the finest, most steadfast courage is shown by Bunyan when he faces the thought of a death that might—so apprehensive is he still—be without any sign of God's comfort at the last:

> It was my duty to stand to his word, whether he would ever look upon me or no, or save me at the last: wherefore, thought I, the point being thus, I am for going on, and venturing my eternal state with Christ, whether I have comfort here or no; if God doth not come in, thought I, I will leap off the ladder even blindfold into eternity, sink or swim, come heaven, come hell, Lord Jesus, if thou wilt catch me, do; if not, I will venture for thy name. (p. 100)

Actually he was called upon to suffer nothing more dramatic than imprisonment, but this was prolonged for years, partly owing to his poverty. He had married a second wife in 1659, his first having died in the previous year, and there is a verbatim account, taken down by Bunyan, of how Elizabeth pleaded for her husband's release before Sir Matthew Hale and other justices in 1661. Among her arguments was the economic one: Bunyan, she said, desired to live peaceably and follow his calling, that his family might be maintained; and she went on to say:

> My lord, I have four small children that cannot help themselves, of which one is blind, and have nothing to live upon, but the charity of good people.
>
> Hast thou four children? said Judge Hale; thou art but a young woman to have four children.
>
> My lord, said she, I am but mother-in-law to them, having not been married to him yet full two years. Indeed, I was with child when my husband was first apprehended; but being young, and unaccustomed to such things, said she, I being smayed with the news, fell into labour, and so continued for eight days, and then was delivered, but my child died.

Whereat, he looking very soberly on the matter, said, Alas, poor woman!

But Judge Twisdon told her, that she made poverty her cloak; and said, moreover, that he understood I was maintained better by running up and down a-preaching, than by following my calling.

What is his calling? said Judge Hale.

Then some of the company that stood by said, A tinker, my lord.

Yes, said she, and because he is a tinker and a poor man, therefore he is despised, and cannot have justice.

Then Judge Hale answered, very mildly, saying, I tell thee, woman . . . thou must either apply thyself to the king or sue out his pardon, or get a writ of error. (p. 126)

But all these courses would have been far too costly for a tinker's family to pursue. For twelve years, with brief intermissions, Bunyan remained in Bedford Gaol, earning a little money by making tagged laces, but principally devoting himself to writing. Among the many books written during this period of imprisonment, the most remarkable is *Grace Abounding*. He was not cut off from visitors, and his fortitude much increased his local reputation. When he finally was released in 1672 under the Declaration of Indulgence, he was appointed pastor of Bedford Meeting and became the organiser of Baptist activities for the whole district.

In 1677 he suffered another term of imprisonment, though only a brief one; and it is with this period in prison that *Pilgrim's Progress* is associated. It had an immediate success when it appeared in 1678, and Bunyan's reputation instead of being merely local became national and even international, since the book was translated before his death into Welsh, French and Dutch. *The Life and Death of Mr Badman* followed in 1680, *The Holy War* in 1682, and the second part of *The Pilgrim's Progress* in 1684. The popularity of his books and his own personal fame caused him to be greatly in demand as a preacher, and it was on one of his horseback journeys to preach in London that he got soaked to the skin and caught the chill of which he died on 31st August 1688.

Grace Abounding covers only the first thirty-two years of Bunyan's life, and with great tracts of time and circumstance, even within this span, he is not in the least concerned. Human happenings seemed comparatively insignificant to John Bunyan as, from Bedford Gaol, he reviewed the crucial drama of his life, the struggle for his soul between God and the devil. The story had come to a triumphant conclusion, and the proof of abounding grace was clear for all to see. It was no longer a matter of purely personal conviction, for during his days as a lay-preacher he had been a chosen representative of the local Baptists, and now as a prisoner he was far more gloriously their representative. Yet if he had been minded to write a narrative of his domestic and active life, he could have produced a wonderfully lively and fascinating social document. His powers of minute observation, his memory for effective detail and his mastery of dialogue, later to be used so effectively in *The Pilgrim's Progress* and *Mr Badman*, can already be seen in *Grace Abounding*. Only occasionally, however, does he employ them to record human episodes. There is nothing more touching, or more revealing of the man's best qualities, than his account of his distress at being separated from his family at the time of his imprisonment, and his especial anxiety for his poor blind child, who lay nearer to his heart than all he had besides. We get another glimpse of his domestic life when he tells how his wife's premature labour pains were once arrested as if in answer to his prayer. But details of this kind are alien to his main purpose, which is to relate the dealings of God with his soul.

The contrast between his present and his former state must

have appeared in very strong and positive colours to Bunyan in prison. He need not be accused of insincerity when he bestows upon himself the title of 'chief of sinners', even if this was a distinction to which many Puritans, Cromwell among them, laid claim, thus exposing themselves to the charge of cant. Those who had undergone painful, prolonged or spectacular conversions were naturally prone to denounce their former selves as filthy wretches in order to magnify the goodness of God; for they never claimed that their new-found righteousness was due to their own efforts, nor expected any credit for it; the praise was due to God alone. Even though Bunyan's insistence on the depravity of his childhood and youth may have been to some extent conventional—it is a feature common to most conversion-narratives—we need not infer from this that he was deliberately distorting autobiographical facts. He could only see the past through the lens of the theology he had adopted. The contrast, to their own consciences, between reprobate sinners and elected saints was so momentous, so immensely fraught with eternal consequences, that seventeenth-century Calvinists could, without conscious exaggeration, describe their psychological experiences in terms that today seem not only archaic but hysterical. Yet this language, as used by Bunyan, does not ring false. His self-abasement is never hypocritical nor his raptures faked. If, in retrospect, the whole process of his conversion appears to him almost miraculous, the record of his heroic life and his large output of books are there to witness to the truth of what he contended —that he did, by grace, get the better of the recurrent temptation to believe himself damned.

All the evidence in *Grace Abounding* suggests that John Bunyan was in his youth an extraordinarily impressionable and unbalanced person. The psychopathic elements in his make-up, and their effect on his particular type of conversion, were pointed out long ago by William James,[1] and the author of *Mark Rutherford*, himself well qualified to sympathise with religious sufferings, describes the book as 'a terrible story of the mental struggle of a man of genius of a peculiarly nervous and almost hypochondriacal temperament, whose sufferings, though they are intertwisted with Puritanism, have roots that lie deep in our common nature'.[2]

Even as a little boy John Bunyan was terrified by fearful dreams and dreadful visions, and the terror of hell-fire afflicted him when he was at play. Though he outgrew these dreams, he remained exceptionally sensitive. In the course of describing himself as a hardened sinner, he unwittingly reveals how far from hardened he was when he lets fall the reminiscence that when he heard a reputedly religious man swearing 'It had so great a stroke upon my spirit, that it made my heart to ache'. The phraseology is characteristic; Bunyan habitually describes psychological states in vividly physical terms. Not only were his spiritual agonies accompanied by violent bodily agitations; his dream symbolism often has a startlingly physical quality. As an example of the almost epileptic state into which his worst temptations drove him, we have his account of the time when the compulsion to sin against the Holy Ghost made him 'ready to clap my hand under my chin, to hold my mouth from opening; and to that end also I have had thoughts at other times, to leap with my head downward into some muck-hill or other, to keep my mouth from speaking.' (p. 34) But not less remarkable in its way is his dream of regeneration, expressed in terms which so closely correspond to the experience of physical birth:

About this time, the state and happiness of these poor people at Bedford was thus, in a dream or vision, represented to me. I saw,

[1] *The Varieties of Religious Experience*, 1902.
[2] W. Hale White, *John Bunyan*, 1905, p. 9.

as if they were set on the sunny side of some high mountain, there refreshing themselves with the pleasant beams of the sun, while I was shivering and shrinking in the cold, afflicted with frost, snow, and dark clouds. Methought, also, betwixt me and them, I saw a wall that did compass about this mountain; now, through this wall my soul did greatly desire to pass; concluding, that if I could, I would go even into the very midst of them, and there also comfort myself with the heat of their sun.

About this wall I thought myself, to go again and again, still prying as I went, to see if I could find some way in or passage, by which I might enter therein; but none could I find for some time. At last, I saw, as it were, a narrow gap, like a little doorway in the wall, through which I attempted to pass; but the passage being very strait and narrow, I made many efforts to get in, but all in vain, even until I was well-nigh quite beat-out, by striving to get in; at last, with great striving, methought I at first did get in my head, and after that, with a sidling striving, my shoulders, and my whole body; then was I exceedingly glad, and went and sat down in the midst of them, and so was comforted with the light and heat of their sun. (p. 21)

'With a sidling striving'—the phrase is so vivid as to be almost painful; and though Bunyan's instinct for imagery deeply rooted in common physical experience stood him in good stead both in *Grace Abounding* and in *Pilgrim's Progress*, the relation of religious experiences in such unselfconscious terms can be disquieting in a way that he never could have suspected. It is impossible to read *Grace Abounding* and not marvel that Bunyan retained his sanity.

Then was I struck into a very great trembling, insomuch that at sometimes I could, for whole days together, feel my very body, as well as my mind, to shake and totter under the sense of the dreadful judgement of God, that should fall on those that have sinned that most fearful and unpardonable sin. I felt also such a clogging and heat at my stomach, by reason of this my terror, that I was in, especially at some times, as if my breast bone would have split in sunder; then thought I of that concerning Judas,

who, by his falling headlong, burst asunder, and all his bowels
gushed out. . . . Thus did I wind, and twine, and shrink, under
the burden that was upon me; which burden also did so oppress
me, that I could neither stand, nor go, nor lie, either at rest
or quiet. (p. 50)

Christian with his burden at the opening of *Pilgrim's Progress*
is a touching figure whose significance has come home to
thousands of readers; but in *Grace Abounding* Bunyan recalls
with almost unbearable poignancy the actual weight of that
burden on his own shoulders.

The book was written in a mood of thanksgiving, and the
Bedford Baptists no doubt accepted it in the spirit in which it
was offered and derived spiritual encouragement from its
pages. Indeed, it does record a heroic struggle and the ultimate
conquest of despair. Yet the modern reader is likely to find
Grace Abounding an extraordinarily painful book, because the
sufferings it records are so disproportionate to any rational
cause. Bunyan seems to have had no normal standards of
reference by which to judge the heinousness of his offences.
Under the pressure of Calvinist demands, his conscience
became so hypersensitive that the pastimes of his early days
—bell-ringing, playing at tip-cat, dancing on the green—
seemed to him activities fraught with evil and most dangerous
to his immortal soul. A blasphemer he may well have been in
his unregenerate youth; he is fairly circumstantial about this;
but he denies most solemnly that he was ever a fornicator, nor
does he accuse himself of dishonesty or drunkenness, or any
kind of antisocial wrongdoing. To quote Richard Baxter on
the Baptist mentality,[1] 'He is endless in his scruples, afraid lest
he sins in every word he speaketh, and in every look, and every
meal he eateth.'

It is true that only he whose conscience is afflicted is able

[1] *Christian Directory*, p. 313.

to judge subjectively of the seriousness of any offence. What appears a trifle to an insensitive observer may torture someone more scrupulous, and whatever moves a man to remorse is, for that man, a sin. If we are sometimes tempted to dismiss a good deal of puritanical self-accusation as morbid cant, the words of Cromwell will serve as a wholesome admonition: 'Our sorrow is the inverted image of our nobleness. The depth of our despair measures what capability and height of claim we have to hope.'[1]

Nevertheless, there is something morbid in Bunyan's terror at the voice of God which seemed to rebuke him for puerile Sabbath-breaking; something which cannot be wholly explained by the savage theology of which he was a victim. God and man are seen in inappropriate terms. God is reduced to the status of an irrational tyrant, and Bunyan's errors are given a cosmic significance. Bunyan is sometimes regarded as a religious genius, but if his spiritual insight is compared with that of his contemporary, Pascal, the egocentricity of his whole attitude becomes apparent. And if we compare him with a religious genius admittedly by nature self-absorbed, St Augustine, we recognise in the *Confessions* the problems that engage the will and the intellect and the imagination of a fully developed man, whereas in *Grace Abounding* most of the offences that torture Bunyan with a sense of sin sprang from obsessions peculiar to himself.

It was, of course, precisely with the hope of bringing about just such a momentous conversion as Bunyan's that Baptist ministers like Gifford—himself a spectacular example of regeneration—imposed upon enquirers that discipline of relentless self-questioning that can drive a man out of his mind. Calvinist theology inflicts its cruellest terrors on potentially good people—those with tender consciences, the very ones

---

[1] *Letters and Speeches*, ed. Carlyle, 1846, vol. 1, p. 67.

least likely to become vicious. Besides poor ignorant unstable Bunyan, one recalls poor gentle harmless Cowper, driven to intermittent madness by fear of damnation.

Bunyan had no defence against his spiritual anguish and the sense of dereliction that came upon him; no support of sacraments or liturgy, no bulwark of secular education, no distractions of a cultivated environment; he was exposed to sheer agony, and he had to wrestle with it alone. Although he was sometimes able to speak of his condition to the other members of the congregation and to ask for their prayers, he seems to have been able to derive but little comfort from them. 'The people of God . . . would pity me, and would tell me of the promises; but they had as good have told me that I must reach the sun with my finger as have bidden me to receive or rely upon the promise.' (p. 27) 'An Ancient Christian', to whom he confided his fear that he had committed the sin against the Holy Ghost, told him that he thought he had. 'Here therefore, I had but cold comfort,' said Bunyan; but he turned again to wrestle in the spirit.

It is significant that when Bunyan did at long last receive assurance that his sins had been forgiven and that Christ had indeed redeemed him, he exclaims, 'Now I could look from myself to Him.' It was his inability to do that, for more than brief moments, that made his time of trial so appallingly lonely. Baxter remarks of the Baptists, 'All their thoughts are contracted and turned inward on themselves: self-troubling is the sum of their thoughts and lives.'[1]

As Bunyan grappled with the whole momentous issue of salvation, the nervous instability which had made his childhood wretched with dreams and horrors reasserted itself. He relied exclusively upon his feelings. When intellectual doubts assailed him, as they occasionally did, he quickly abandoned any

[1] *Christian Directory*, p. 313.

attempt to conquer them by argument and eventually trusted his instincts.

> Everyone doth think his own religion rightest, both Jews and Moors, and Pagans! and how if all our faith, and Christ, and Scriptures, be but a think-so too? Sometimes I have endeavoured to argue against these suggestions, and to set some of the sentences of blessed Paul against them; but alas! I quickly felt, when I thus did, such arguings as these would return again upon me. . . . These suggestions, with many other which at this time I may not, nor dare not utter, neither by word nor pen, did make such a seizure upon my spirit, and did so overweigh my heart . . . that I felt as if there were nothing else but these from morning to night within me; and as though, indeed, there could be room for nothing else; and also concluded that God had, in very wrath to my soul, given me up unto them, to be carried away with them, as with a mighty whirlwind. Only by the distaste that they gave unto my spirit, I felt that there was something in me that refused to embrace them. (p. 32)

Characteristically, it is all expressed in terms of sensation. His reluctance to use his reason was partly responsible for the two years of excruciating misery that he suffered when he thought he had committed the sin of Judas; for he admits that when at length he brought himself to 'go another way to work, even to consider the nature of this blasphemous thought', he came at last to the conclusion that he had not, in fact, betrayed his Lord when he had breathed the words, 'Let Him go if He will.'

Quite irrational, too, is his utter dependence upon random texts from the Bible. A superstitious pagan, believing in oracles and portents, was not more at their mercy than the pious Bunyan haunted by passages from Holy Writ. In this he was not peculiar. Hooker, long before his day, had pointed out the folly of tearing biblical texts from their settings and using them as oracles: 'What shall the Scriptures be but a snare and

torment to weak consciences, filling them with infinite per-
plexities, scrupulosities, doubts insoluble and extreme despairs.'[1]
But zealous Protestants, who gave an equal weight and significance to every word of the Bible, continued to be exposed to
these miseries. If Baxter had known of Bunyan's case he could
not have summed it up more cogently than in his comment on
'mistaken Christians' who 'are between terrours and comforts
distracted by their own fantasies, and think it all done by the
Spirit of God'.[2]

Bunyan's spiritual sufferings have to be set in their historical
context, for a host of Baptists, Quakers, Ranters and Muggle-
tonians were undergoing similar agonies and revelations in
this extraordinary period of religious 'enthusiasm'. Many have
left written records of their conversions, and nearly all must
have given verbal testimony of the inner struggles that preceded their assurance of salvation. The archives of Bunyan's
own Bedford Meeting confirm that an aspirant to membership
had to give to the faithful an account of the work of grace
upon his heart before he could be admitted, and Bunyan
himself must have testified some years before he wrote the full
story in *Grace Abounding*. But when all has been done to
discount the originality of the book, its poignancy remains.

It was the pressure of a peculiar Protestant convention that
forced him to unburden himself in print of matters which a
Catholic might have confided to his spiritual director; but it
was his own integrity that gave the record its intensely moving
and individual quality. Though Bunyan was not motivated by
the normal kind of egocentricity that prompts a man to self-
portraiture, and though he disregarded whole tracts of his own
human experience, he did produce in *Grace Abounding* an
authentic picture of himself during his years of crisis. He

[1] *Ecclesiastical Polity*, Bk. II, ch. 8, par. 6.
[2] *The Life of Faith*, quoted by H. Martin, *Puritanism and Richard Baxter*, 1954.

revealed, indeed, far more than he intended. It is the un-conscious exposure of weaknesses that gives to the whole book an undertone of pain that perhaps was not audible to its original readers, accustomed as they were to Puritan exhibi-tionism. He wrote to strengthen and encourage his brethren, not to indulge any taste for self-analysis. Yet the unspoken motive of confessional autobiographers, the longing for relief in pouring out pent-up memories, must have worked very strongly with Bunyan. Though he was not wholly cut off from the society of his fellows, he was in prison when he wrote *Grace Abounding*, deprived of the companionship of his wife and children, thrown back upon his own thoughts. The need to communicate, to establish a bond of sympathy between himself and those from whom he was separated, may have given to *Grace Abounding* its characteristic tone of passionate frankness.

Richard Baxter

❧❀❧

During his lifetime Richard Baxter was known throughout England as one of the foremost spokesmen of the Puritan party within the Church. His *Saints' Everlasting Rest* was among the most widely read books of the seventeenth century, and the weight of his polemical writings, together with the centrality of his position, made him a formidable man to reckon with at the Restoration. He was so famed for his piety and pertinacity that he could argue with Oliver Cromwell about the dangers of sectarianism in the army and commonwealth, plead with Charles II for toleration towards the nonconforming clergy, twice refuse a bishopric, present his reforming schemes to the Savoy Conference, and be mercilessly abused in his old age when brought to trial before Judge Jeffreys. Fervently religious, with a powerful intellect, he was drawn (not wholly against his will) into public affairs; he was one of the most renowned preachers in England; but in his own estimation his writings were the most important part of his labours. For years he was a persecuted man, for most of his life a sick and suffering one; but no affliction could break his spirit or silence his pen. His published works number one hundred and sixty-eight. Very few of them are ever opened nowadays, even by students of theological controversy in seventeenth-century England. That his name is still known and honoured is due to the life that he led and the person that he was.

As an ageing man, Baxter wrote his memoirs, a 'Narrative

of the Most Memorable Passages of his Life and Times.' This appeared in 1696, five years after his death, as *Reliquiae Baxterianae*. All his literary remains had been entrusted to his devoted but rather inept friend Matthew Sylvester, whose reverence for Baxter prevented him from bringing good order into the chaos of papers that he had to deal with. Edmund Calamy, another staunch friend of Baxter, and himself a leading Puritan divine, published in 1702 what he called an *Abridgement* of the *Reliquiae Baxterianae*; but if Sylvester had erred through diffidence, Calamy exceeded an editor's prerogative, by re-writing Baxter's first-person narrative in the third-person, 'improving' his often homely diction and making some unwarrantable cuts. The book became effectively available to the general reader only in 1925, when Mr J. M. Lloyd Thomas produced his excellent abridgement, published in the Everyman Library as *The Autobiography of Richard Baxter*.[1]

Here we have a life-history at once wider and more analytical than any we have so far considered. It is the record of an eminent man—far more influential in his own day than Browne the country doctor, or Herbert the discredited ambassador, or even than the Baptist tinker who was known in his latter days as 'Bishop Bunyan', and whose *Pilgrim's Progress* was read in his own lifetime beyond the bounds of Britain. And this eminent man was concerned with the double task of reporting the outward circumstances of his life and times and of analysing his development as a Christian soul. So it is that we find in Baxter's *Autobiography* a word-portrait of Oliver Cromwell that can be set beside the 'character' composed by Clarendon, and descriptions of the Plague and the Great Fire that supplement the first-hand accounts of Pepys and Evelyn. At the same time, his Self-Analysis is far more

[1] Page references are to this edition.

subtle and perspicacious than the testimonies of the average soul-searching Puritans and Quakers.

Baxter's autobiography has no claim to be called a work of art; but students of history and of human psychology are equally in his debt, since the book combines the factual interest of memoirs with some extraordinarily sober and balanced self-examination. Baxter has none of the fantasy of Sir Thomas Browne, but he shares his deep interest in idiosyncrasy and personal development. He has none of Lord Herbert's frivolity, but resembles him in his appreciation of the importance of factual detail in a personal chronicle, and in his easy handling of public events. Like John Bunyan, he believes in the supreme importance of individual salvation and in the duty of sharing religious experiences, but unlike him he is reticent about his own 'particular mercies', presenting instead of a conversion-drama an inclusive review of his whole life, which suggests, if it does not overtly assert, the significance to the growth of the soul of such factors as personal relationships, health, intellectual interests and the larger movements of history.

Baxter's account of his boyhood reveals his memory for telling detail and his strong sense of cause and effect. We are shown the sobriety of his solidly unpretentious home in Shropshire against a background of country ignorance, superstition and jollity. He censures himself sharply for his youthful follies, which included a liking (and in this he resembled St Augustine) for stolen fruit. In retrospect he blames himself for having as a boy been 'extremely bewitched by a love of romances, fables and old tales', but he never lost his love for poetry, and reading remained throughout his life a passion. He was too delicate to receive much formal education, and never went to the university, but he compensated this lack by devouring books, especially volumes of divinity, metaphysics and logic. Significantly, he notes the attraction which the Schoolmen exercised upon his growing mind:

> because I thought they narrowly searched after truth, and brought things out of the darkness of confusion; for I could never from my first studies endure confusion. . . . I never thought I could understand anything till I could anatomise it and see the parts distinctly, and the conjunction of the parts as they made up the whole. (*Autobiography*, p. 10)

It was this analytical bent that stood Baxter in such good stead when he came to write his own life-history.

Our judgement of his qualities as an autobiographer must not be based on his posthumous work alone. In 1681 he published, on the death of his wife, a *Breviate of the Life of Margaret . . . Wife of Richard Baxter*,[1] which not only pays a devoted and beautiful tribute to her memory but movingly admits the reader to the life that he shared with her for nineteen years. In the same year, prompted by grief, he also published his *Poetical Fragments*, among which is to be found an incomplete autobiography in verse.[2]

In spite of his genuine humility, Baxter was not unaware that he was an exceptional man, and he knew that certain aspects of his private life would be of interest and profit to others. There was an immense interchange of edifying personal reminiscences among the Puritans, and it is against this background that Baxter's autobiographical writings must be set.

Not only were personal testimonies before the faithful required of converts who had discovered in themselves the signs of election; they were also encouraged to keep spiritual diaries, in which they noted the further workings of the law of predestination in their souls. John Janeway, one of the many

---

[1] Ed. with introduction and notes by J. T. Wilkinson, 1928.
[2] My page references are to the fourth edition (Pickering), 1821.

diarists quoted by William Haller in *The Rise of Puritanism*[1] was accustomed to note

> What incomes and profit he received in his spiritual traffique; what returns from that far-country; what answers of prayer; what deadness and flatness, and what observable providences did present themselves, and the substance of what he had been doing; and any wanderings of thoughts, inordinancy in any passions; which though the world could not discern, he could.

Sometimes these diaries were in shorthand, but some from their literary style were evidently composed with one eye on eventual readers. There was a strong congregational sense among the Puritans which encouraged them to feel concern and curiosity about their neighbours' spiritual symptoms, over and above the intense introspective care which they lavished on their own.

One of the reasons which Baxter gave for publishing the life of his wife was that truthful biographies of good Christians serve to edify their fellows; and one of his reasons, though not the foremost, for making public his own 'Self-Analysis and Life Review' was

> ... that young Christians may be warned by the mistakes and failings of my unriper times, to learn in patience, and live in watchfulness, and not be fierce and proudly confident in their first conceptions, and to reverence ripe experienced age, and to take heed of taking such for their chief guides as have nothing but immature and unexperienced judgments, with fervent affections, and free and confident expressions; but to learn of them that have with holiness, study, time and trial, looked about them as well on one side as the other, and attained to clearness and impartiality in their judgments. (*Autobiography*, p. 129)

Since the Reformation, Protestants could no longer enjoy the innumerable Saints' Lives that had been the staple

[1] Columbia University Press, 1938, p. 100.

'improving reading' of medieval Englishmen, but the popularity of Foxe's *Book of Martyrs* indicates that taste had not greatly changed. Funeral sermons, which usually included a biographical sketch of the deceased, were often reprinted and eagerly read. Donne's beautiful tribute to the memory of Magdalen Herbert is a fine specimen of memorial biography, and Baxter himself made several essays in this field. In his wife's will, she begged him to reprint five hundred copies of the funeral sermon that he had composed for her mother; and in the same year as he wrote the *Breviate* for his wife, he celebrated his own step-mother, who had lived in great piety to the age of ninety-six, and also his

> ... old friend and housekeeper, Jane Matthews, who lived in pious, humble virginity, with eminent worth, to about seventy-six or seventy-seven years, and died of mere decay, without considerable pain or sickness, about a month or six weeks before my wife.[1]

Samuel Clark, a trusted friend of Baxter's who officiated at his marriage, compiled several volumes to satisfy the Puritan demand for edifying biographies, one of which contains an abridgement of the life of Margaret Baxter, together with a preface by Baxter himself.

Baxter's *Breviate*, then, falls into the immediately recognisable category of edifying biography, and a good deal of his own life-history, though written in the first person singular, can be classed under the same heading. The *Breviate* includes a number of Margaret Baxter's private expressions of religious faith, which give it something of the quality of a Spiritual Diary; this too we find in the *Autobiography*. But the long sections of that book concerned with public events recall rather Bishop Burnet's *History of My Own Times*, or the more or less

[1] *Breviate*, ed. J. T. Wilkinson, p. 62. All page references are to this edition.

contemporary diaries of Evelyn, Sir John Reresby or Pepys (in his capacity as an observer of historical events).

Because Baxter was a man of eminence, whose personal Christian life was intimately affected by those political changes (such as the Act of Uniformity) which involved changes in church government, and because he himself exercised a great influence in just these religio-political matters, he was constrained to combine a history of his times with that of his life. Indeed, there is more gratuitous historical information and less confessional detail in his memoirs than might be expected. But it was impossible for such a nationally known figure to keep public and private themes apart.

To some extent the *Autobiography* is a vindication of Baxter's career. He admits that one of his motives in writing his life was 'to prevent the defective performance of this task by some overvaluing brethren, who I know intended it and were unfitter to do it than I myself', and that he also wished to defend his reputation against detractors. (p. 129) He had already had ample experience of calumny and in his old age was exposed to persistent persecution. Yet the *Autobiography*, in spite of being the personal vindication of a man who in his day had not spared his opponents in controversy, is not at all defiant in tone. It is always fair-minded and generally charitable. Baxter's fierce polemics had inspired respect rather than love in those who did not know him well; but his autobiography is the ripest fruit of his long experience of life, the book of a man both wise and good.

What indications are to be found of Baxter's qualities as an autobiographer in the *Breviate* and the *Poetical Fragments*, those two glimpses into his private life which he vouchsafed to the public ten years before his death? Both books reveal a strong impulse to talk about himself and his intimate concerns —that confidingness which is perhaps the most essential of all autobiographical requisites. The surge of emotion released by the shock of his wife's death (she was much younger than he) was something that needed to be shared. The *Breviate* was the immediate expression of his grief; and this unusually expansive mood prompted Baxter to make public the verses which for the most part had been composed years earlier. He was not habitually an unreserved man, and the tension between his strong emotion and his customary reticence is clearly to be seen in the addresses to the readers which he prefixed to each book. Introducing the *Poetical Fragments*, he explains:

> God having taken away the dear companion of the last nineteen years of my life, as her sorrows and sufferings long ago gave being to some of these Poems (for reasons which the world is not concerned to know) so my grief for her removal, and the revived sense of former things, have prevailed with me to be passionate in the open sight of all.   (p. 1)

There is a similar defence of passion, yet with a touch of apology for a lack of manly reserve, in his preface to the *Breviate*. He confesses that the book was written 'under the power of melting Grief, and therefore perhaps with the less prudent judgment; but not with the less, but with the more Truth: for passionate weakness poureth out all, which greater Prudence may conceal.' (p. 61) There is a wry humour in his admission that 'Affection makes us think our own or our friends' affairs to be such as the world should be affected with: I perceive this weakness and submit. . . .' (p. 65)

Baxter may indeed have slackened, under the pressure of intense emotion, his customarily tight hold upon himself, but neither distress nor tenderness are to be allowed to distort his truthfulness. The opening paragraph of the *Breviate* runs:

> Though due affection make me willing to give the world a narrative which else I had omitted; yet the fear of God hath not

so forsaken me, that I should willingly deliver any falsehood through partiality or passion: but as I knew more of this person than of any other, for the good of the readers and the honour of God's grace in her, I shall by God's assistance truly report the things which I know. (p. 67)

Here is revealed one of Baxter's finest qualities as an auto-biographer—his immense and unfailing reverence for truth. This was the quality in him which particularly struck Coleridge, who observed with reference to the narrative of his life and times,

I may not infrequently doubt Baxter's memory, or even his competence, in consequence of his particular modes of thinking; but I could almost as soon doubt the Gospel verity as his veracity. ... Under ... accursed persecutions he feels and reasons more like an angel than a man.[1]

The third characteristic of a good autobiographer that is made manifest in the *Breviate* is psychological penetration. The book is a closely-observed character-study of Margaret Charlton, who became Baxter's wife when he was forty-seven and she twenty-six. The delightful account that Baxter gives of their married life, which necessarily familiarises us with him as well as with her, is only incidental to his main purpose, which is to let us watch the development of her Christian character. When as a girl of nineteen she first came to Kidderminster, where Baxter was exerting a powerful influence as preacher and pastor of souls, she 'had great aversion to the poverty and strictness of the people there, glittering herself in costly apparel and delighting in her romances'. (p. 70) But her mother was renowned for her piety, and when Margaret came under Baxter's spell, 'she presently fell to self-judging and to frequent prayer and serious thoughts'. During a serious illness, the prayers of the congregation were fervent

[1] *Notes on English Divines*, 1853, vol. ii, p. 68.

for her recovery, and her thorough conversion was a matter for their thanksgiving. In sickness and distress, Baxter was her spiritual adviser. In the *Breviate* he prints certain private papers, full of heart-searchings, that he himself had never seen before her death, together with counsels of his own on various spiritual topics, that she had transcribed. Several times Baxter mentions her extreme reserve; 'she kept all matters so secret to herself, as was her great hurt all her life'. For fear of hypocrisy she was most reluctant to speak in public on religious matters, deeply though she cared about them. Her integrity of spirit and the intensity of her fervour come out in her private papers; and the difficulty which she evidently felt in unburdening her heart to Baxter while she was as yet only his convert may perhaps be explained by the fact that she loved him but had to keep her love concealed. Certainly after marriage she blossomed into a new and radiant cheerfulness, and readily adapted herself to all the hardships which she met with as the wife of an ejected minister. Though she was delicate and easily frightened, she showed herself an admirable counsellor, a woman of great practical ability and an excellent housekeeper.

> Her household affairs she ordered with so great skill and decency, as that others much praised that which I was no fit judge of. I had been bred among plain, mean people, and I thought that so much washing of stairs and rooms, to keep them as clean as their trenchers and dishes, and so much ado about cleanliness and trifles, was a sinful curiosity and expense of servants' time, who might that while have been reading some good book. But she that was otherwise bred had other thoughts. (p. 137)

Margaret came of the landed gentry, Baxter of yeoman stock; but he was so much older and more experienced and wiser than she that the social inequality counted for nothing. Baxter dwells particularly on her generosity, her quick and sound judgement and her long-suffering spirit. Though he clearly was deeply devoted to her, the tone of the *Breviate* is not adulatory but tenderly reminiscent. His own faults and foibles come in for severer censure than hers, but he makes no plaster saint of her.

> She was of an extraordinary sharp and piercing wit. She had a natural reservedness and secrecy, increased by thinking it necessary prudence not to be open; by which means she was often misunderstood by her nearest friends, and consequently often crost and disappointed by those that would have pleased her. And as she could understand men much by their looks and hints, so she expected all should know her mind without expressing it, which bred her frustrations and discontents. (p. 128)

The fifth chapter described her 'temper' or bodily constitution —'The soul while in the body works much according to the bodies disposition'—and the eighth gives a careful account of her 'mental qualifications and infirmities'. The utter sincerity of Baxter's assessment makes the portrait far more vivid and touching than any artifice of flattery could contrive.

The subtlety of observation which pervades the whole of the *Breviate* is also conspicuous in the *Autobiography*. There are some 'characters' here which can be matched with Clarendon's; the portraits of Oliver Cromwell, for example, or Sir Matthew Hale, or that Puritan worthy, old Mr Simeon Ash, who 'seasonably went to heaven at the very time when he was to be cast out of the church'. (p. 186) Most notably, however, Baxter's psychological penetration is displayed in his Self-Analysis, which is the very core of the *Autobiography*. Sir James Stephen, admitting that *Reliquiae Baxterianae* as a whole was an unwieldy great book, called this section of it 'the most impressive record in our language . . . of the gradual ripening of a powerful mind under the culture of incessant study, wide experience and anxious self-observation'.[1]

[1] *Essays in Ecclesiastical Biography*, 1849, vol. ii, p. 60.

Only a man with a natural inclination towards autobiography would have conceived the project, which Baxter
executed in part, of versifying his life-history. He was obliged
to abandon it in the midst of the Civil Wars, and in his old
age had no heart to finish the poem that he personally considered his best. It is a recital of the most notable mercies of his
life, enclosed within a hymn of thanksgiving to God for all his
love and mercy to the world in general. *Love breathing Thanks
and Praise* is very far from being a poetical masterpiece, but
autobiographically it is interesting, for in it Baxter traces the
outlines of his career as well as his spiritual development. It
gets off to a bad start:

> Eternal God! this worm lifts up the head,
> And looks to thee, by thee encouraged . . .
> If thou vouchsafe to make a worm rejoice,
> Give him a thankful praising heart and voice . . .
>
> *(Poetical Fragments, p. 1)*

but this is followed by an eloquent passage on the attributes of
God and man's desire to know Him. The second section deals
with Baxter's youth, and epitomises material which we find in
the prose *Autobiography*. These lines about his boyhood errors
will serve to indicate the general level:

> Yet sin sprung up and early did appear
> In love of play, and lies produced by fear;
> An appetite pleased with forbidden fruit,
> A proud delight in literate repute;
> Excess of pleasure in vain tales, romances;
> Time spent in feigned histories and fancies;
> In idle talk, conform to company . . . (p. 9)

Yet there are occasional images and echoes that remind us that
Baxter loved George Herbert above any other poet:

> Thy methods cross'd my ways; my young desire
> To academic glory did aspire . . . (p. 37)

or, of the pastoral work at Kidderminster,

> Mercies grew thicker there than summer-flowers . . .
> (p. 40)

There are even passages that recall the ardent devotional flights of Crashaw:

> At every mention of thy blessed name,
> My ravish'd soul should mount up in love's flame . . .
> And when my Lord's love-sufferings I read,
> My pierced and love-wounded heart should bleed.
> Love should enforce each word when I do pray;
> A flaming heart I'd on thy altar lay:
> When halving hypocrites give thee a part,
> Love should present my whole, though broken, heart . . .
> (p. 15)

If the Counter-reformation quality of the imagery seems surprising in so staunch a Puritan as Baxter, it must be remembered that he was much concerned to foster the practice of systematic meditative prayer, and that having studied the Catholic exponents of meditation he could say, in *The Saints' Everlasting Rest*, 'Learn better the way of Devotion from a Papist.'[1]

Besides the rhymed life-history, there are other autobiographical verses in *Poetical Fragments*, notable among them being 'The Resolution', dated 3rd December 1663—'Written when I was silenced and cast out'. This contains the lines which are used as the hymn, 'He wants not friends that hath Thy love,' and it is in its totality a fine expression of a Christian's dependence upon God. Reflecting that Christ himself suffered wrongful accusation and a travesty of justice, Baxter observes, with an honest simplicity,

---

[1] See an interesting chapter on Baxter in *The Poetry of Meditation*, Louis L. Martz, Yale U.P., 1954.

> It's no great matter what men deem,
>   Whether they count me good or bad;
> In their applause and best esteem
>   There's no contentment to be had.
> I stand not to the bar of man;
>   It's Thy displeasure makes me sad.   (p. 45)

He allows himself a passing regret for his losses:

> Must I be driven from my books,
>   From house, and goods, and dearest friends?   (p. 47)

but then he reflects:

> My Lord hath taught me how to want
>   A place wherein to put my head.   (p. 47)

He foresees what in fact came to pass, sojourns in prison; but reminds himself

> No walls or bars can keep Thee out,
>   None can confine a holy soul:
> The streets of Heav'n it walks about;
>   None can its liberty control.   (p. 49)

In the Preface to *Poetical Fragments* Baxter mentions with approbation Sir John Davies and his poem *Nosce Teipsum*, and among his own verse there is a poem entitled *Man* that certainly owes much to it both in form and content. Like Davies, Baxter asks the question that since the Renaissance had never ceased to trouble men of lively intelligence:

> Vain Man! why is thy being no more known?
> Why, seeking knowledge, read'st thou not thyself?
> How many books in vain dost thou take down?
> Thy own book standeth on the nearest shelf.   (p. 153)

In this and other poems Baxter emphasises the vileness of the flesh with morbid particularity, but his sense of man's high destiny impels him to a couple of fine stanzas:

> If all men made themselves, and are their own,
> And have no ruler but self-will and sense;
> If man be nothing else but flesh and bone,
> Can live here still, and say, I'll go not hence;
>
> If man can conquer God, and him dethrone,
> Kill Christ again, and shut up Paradise;
> Then saints are fools, and worldly men alone,
> Choosing a shadow and despair, are wise.   (p. 161)

It is only as a hymn-writer that Baxter has earned any kind of poetical fame. 'Ye holy angels bright' comes from one of his poems, and the hymn 'Lord, it belongs not to my care' is taken from a poem summarising his wife's 'covenant' at the time of her conversion; an expression of absolute trust in God, as well in adversity as in happiness, containing the memorable verse:

> Christ leads me through no darker rooms
>   Than he went through before;
> He that into God's kingdom comes
>   Must enter by this door.   (p. 72)

Baxter knew well enough that his poetical gifts did not amount to much, yet he cared for poetry, and for music too. The preface to his *Poetical Fragments* gives some valuable sidelights on his tastes. Unlike some of his Puritan brethren, he delights in church music, and has constantly defended it against objectors. 'I confess that harmony and melody are the pleasure and elevation of my soul.' (p. iii) As for poetry, 'Sure, there is somewhat of heaven in Holy Poetry. It charmeth souls with loving harmony and concord.' (p. v) Moreover, 'These times have produced many excellent poets.' Among those whom he singles out for commendation, besides Davies,

are Cowley, Katherine Philips ('the matchless Orinda'),
Wither, Quarles, Fulke Greville and George Sandys. But it is
to George Herbert that he gives the highest praise, and his
love and admiration are based on that penetrating understanding which is expressed in the well-known judgement,
'Herbert speaks to God like one that really believeth a God,
and whose business in this world is most with God. Heart-
work and Heaven-work make up his books.' (p. iv)

The very title-page of Baxter's book of poems brings to
mind Herbert's divine colloquies: 'Poetical Fragments.
Heart-Imployment with GOD and ITSELF. The Con-
cordant Discord of a Broken-healed Heart. Sorrowing-
rejoicing, fearing-hoping, dying-living. . . . Published for the
Use of the Afflicted.' The peroration to the preface, too, is one
that Herbert would not have disowned: 'The Lord by his
merciful providence and his grace, tune up our dull and
drooping souls to such joyful praises, as may prepare us for
his everlasting praise in Heaven. London, at the Door of
Eternity, August 7, 1681.' (But poor Baxter had to wait at that
Door, lonely, sick, deprived of all but the barest necessities, for
ten more years.)

The *Poetical Fragments* and the *Breviate*, then, are valuable
auxiliaries to the *Autobiography*, revealing as they do Baxter's
emotional warmth. This indeed makes itself felt in a number of
poignant instances in the full-scale life-history; but here
Baxter's aim was not to unburden himself of private sorrows
and joys, but to give such an account of himself as might
safeguard his reputation against detractors. He was keenly
aware of the significance of the historical events through which
he had lived, and could present his own case as typical of those
innumerable sincere Puritans who could not find it in their
hearts to conform to all the demands of the 'Prelatists',
although they had no wish to join any dissenting sect.

The *Autobiography* falls into three sections. The first, and best-ordered, covers the years 1615–1660. It deals with Baxter's childhood and education, his brief period at Court, his ordination as deacon, his happy years in the ministry that were interrupted by the Civil War, and his resumption, after two years as a chaplain with the Parliamentary forces, of his pastoral charge at Kidderminster. He gives some account of the books he has written, and the personal narrative culminates in his 'Self-Analysis and Life-Review'. But inextricably woven with his own individual story there is the history of England immediately before and during the Civil War and the Protectorate. Baxter gives his own interpretation of the causes that led to the war; he tells of the execution of Charles I and the subsequent battles; he characterises the Westminster Assembly, and gives his estimate of Oliver Cromwell, whom he knew personally. The historical narrative in Part I ends with a caustic account of General Monk's success in restoring a king to the throne of England.

Part II was completed in 1665, when Baxter had been forced by the Great Plague to flee from his house at Acton to take refuge in Buckinghamshire, in the house of the son of John Hampden of Ship-money fame. This section of the narrative covers the period in which Baxter played his most important part in public affairs. For two years after the Restoration he did his best to plead the cause of primitive episcopacy against the entrenched prelatists. At the Savoy Conference, summoned to deal with matters of church discipline, Baxter presented his reformed liturgy (a hasty performance—he had only a fortnight in which to draw it up). He was at the time one of the king's chaplains-in-ordinary, and was offered the bishopric of Hereford, but he refused it rather than compromise with his own conscience or betray the cause of the many Puritan ministers who could not see their way to submitting to the demands of the high-church party. What Baxter ardently desired and toiled for was to mediate between the extremists in English religious life; but like many other peacemakers, he was rewarded only by the distrust of both sides. His account of the various divines at the Conference reveals his shrewdness of observation, though he deliberately refrains from writing 'characters' of them, for fear of betraying an animosity unworthy of a historian, and confines himself to recounting the parts they actually played in the discussions.

In 1662 Baxter was 'silenced and cast out' from the ministry of the Anglican church, along with nearly two thousand other Puritan pastors who could not subscribe to the Act of Uniformity. It was a terrible personal tragedy, but he does not indulge in recriminations or self-pity. Briefly he mentions his marriage and the retired life that he was obliged to lead. Although forbidden to preach, he could and did still write. As though to draw attention away from his own case, and to direct it towards the plight of his brethren, Baxter gives a most interesting review of the different kinds of conformists and non-conformists to be found in England at that time.

This section of the book ends on a note of doom. War with the Dutch, droughts and the threat of famine, comets presaging disaster, and finally,

> The plague hath seized on the famousest and most excellent city of Christendom. . . . It hath scattered and consumed the inhabitants, multitudes being dead and fled. The calamities and cries of the diseased and impoverished are not to be conceived by those that are absent from them. Every man is a terror to his neighbour and himself; for God for our sins is a terror to us all. (p. 191)

Baxter's original intention had been to end the *Narrative of the Most Memorable Passages of his Life and Times* at this point. He could scarcely suppose, after his 'silencing', that the future held any great opportunities of his doing good; and as for his country, he could only, like Milton, reflect on the chances that had been lost. Never, now, would England become 'a land of saints and a pattern of holiness to all the world, and the unmatchable paradise of the earth'. (p. 84) If the plague had carried off Baxter at the age of fifty he would have been spared much misery. But he lived on for another twenty-six years, and twenty-one of them are covered by Part III of the *Autobiography*.

He resumes his narrative with an account of the Great Fire, mentioning with particular grief, good scholar that he was, the terrible loss of books. The booksellers' stocks which had been placed for safety in the vaults of old St Paul's were buried under the weight of falling masonry or caught fire; many libraries of religious books were destroyed. 'I saw the half-burnt leaves of books near my dwelling at Acton, six miles from London,' says Baxter, 'but others found them near Windsor, nearly twenty miles distant.' (p. 199) The havoc within the city itself is recounted in accents of prophetic woe. But the narrative in Part III is far less consecutive than in the planned sections; sometimes it is left in diary form. It tells a sad tale of imprisonments, illnesses and persecutions. Yet though the chronicle becomes more melancholy as Baxter's friends die and leave him a lonely old man, racked with almost constant pain and most cruelly harried by his enemies, it nevertheless mirrors his indomitable spirit.

Historians of the Puritan movement have done justice to Richard Baxter as one of its foremost exponents, both in word and deed, during and just after the Commonwealth period. His importance as a chronicler of his times is also fully recognised. His merits as a pioneer in introspective autobiography, however, had been little noticed. He was not a man given to reminiscence for its own sake, nor a conscious stylist, but he was an uncommonly shrewd analyst both of other men and of himself.

No man is free from delusions about his own nature and motives, but Baxter had trained himself to be freer than most. A man of enormous mental energy and very wide reading, he had in early life learnt from his study of the scholastic philosophers the value of logical analysis, recognising in himself a strongly analytical bent that responded to their methods. It was this capacity for anatomising both arguments and experiences that enabled Baxter to examine his own inner life so dispassionately.

His practical experience, too, during his long ministry at Kidderminster, helped him towards a rare discernment in the treatment of psychological problems. Both from the *Autobiography* and from the *Breviate* it is clear that many people in his charge sought his aid in their spiritual difficulties, and that he encouraged them to do so. Not only during his ministry at Kidderminster, but very much later in his life, after he had been deprived of any chance to officiate within the Church, he was still sought after as a counsellor. Writing of the year 1671, he says,

> I was troubled this year with multitudes of melancholy persons from several parts of the land, some of high quality, some of low, some very exquisitely learned, some unlearned (as I had in a great measure been above twenty years before). I know not how it came to pass, but if men fell melancholy, I must hear from them or see them (more than any physician that I know). .... (p. 216)

This somewhat plaintive remark is followed by a transcript of the counsels that he was accustomed to give his penitents, and these, in their combination of spiritual insight and practical good sense, explain why those in trouble came to him for help. Like his contemporary Jeremy Taylor, Baxter was deeply interested in casuistry; and a study of other men's difficulties of conscience can scarcely fail to refine the powers of self-analysis.

Baxter was wide awake to the perils of introspection and most carefully avoided every temptation to spiritual exhibitionism. An infinitely more sophisticated man than Bunyan, he knew that there were dangers in indulging vulgar curiosity in matters of religious experience, and showed great reserve when he came to write his Life-Review:

> Because it is soul-experiments which those that urge me to this kind of writing do expect that I should especially communicate to others, and I have said little of God's dealing with my soul since the time of my younger years, I shall only give the reader so much satisfaction as to acquaint him truly with what change God hath made upon my mind and heart since those unriper times, and wherein I now differ in judgment and disposition from myself. (p. 103)

It is noteworthy that Baxter gives 'mind' and 'judgement' pre-eminence over 'heart' and 'disposition', and in his self-analysis it is the gradual maturing of his opinions that he traces with scrupulous care. About his growth in grace he speaks diffidently, as though he would have preferred to keep silence. This disinclination is made explicit in the continuation of the introductory remarks quoted above:

> As for any more particular account of heart-occurrences, and God's operations on me, I think it somewhat unsavoury to recite them, seeing God's dealings are much what the same with all his servants in the main, and the points wherein he varieth are usually so small that I think not such fit to be repeated. Nor have I anything extraordinary to glory in which is not common to the rest of my brethren, who have the same spirit and are servants of the same Lord. (p. 103)

His whole approach to the subject of religious experience is by way of a study of the idiosyncrasies of the individual concerned. Unlike the sectarian autobiographers of his day, he did not subordinate all mundane details to the prime purpose of testifying to the workings of the Spirit of God in his own soul. His retrospective review begins with the highly characteristic remark 'The temper of my mind hath somewhat altered with the temper of my body'. Just as in the *Breviate* he pays a good deal of attention to the health and physical constitution of his wife, so he treats of his own. He does not mention their infirmities simply to emphasise how their spirits rose above the limitations of the flesh, but writes with a kind of scientific detachment that recalls Girolamo Cardano.

Baxter's 'Self-Analysis and Life-Review', the very heart of his autobiography, excels in balanced judgement anything known to me in seventeenth-century English writings of this kind. Essentially it is a study of changing attitudes, changing values, changing temper. It might therefore be compared with *Religio Medici*, particularly with the first part, in which Browne sought to account for his present intellectual positions by comparing them with tenets that he had in the course of time abandoned. What Baxter conveys far more powerfully than Browne is the sense of development within an individual man, the steady growth in wisdom that is possible to someone who will learn from experience. It must, of course, be remembered that Browne was only thirty when he wrote *Religio Medici*, whereas Baxter was perhaps twenty years older. He was, besides, a man of immense gravity, quite without Browne's waywardness and humour. But that wisdom is not a matter of years may be demonstrated by a comparison of Baxter with Lord Herbert. Writing in the fulness of his maturity, he regards his earlier self with a critical penetration—not impatient or uncharitable—which was completely lacking in Lord Herbert when at a still more advanced age he looked back on his own youth. Baxter throughout his autobiography, and not only in the central section which is expressly concerned with the assessment of inner development, constantly uses such phrases as 'Yet now I perceive . . .', 'But I understood at last . . .'. The whole book is the fruit of a deeply reflective mind, and one that never ceased to be receptive.

The changes in his own spiritual, intellectual and moral temper which Baxter notes in the course of his Self-analysis are all in the direction of a greater charity. As a young man he had been quick and spirited, a more emotional preacher than in his later years, and a far more vehement controversialist. Experience of life and profounder study have taught him to avoid unnecessary disputations about religion; so much so that he confesses himself

> much prone to the contrary extreme, to be too indifferent what men hold and to keep my judgement to myself and never to mention anything wherein I differ from another, or anything which I think I know more than he; or at least, if he receive it not presently, to silence it, and leave him to his own opinion. (p. 106)

Analysing this disinclination to get involved in religious controversy, Baxter finds that it springs from impatience as well as from a growing concern for peace and concord. He found it very hard to suffer fools gladly, and deplored his own 'impatient temper of mind'.

> I am ready to think that people should quickly understand all in a few words; and if they cannot, lazily to despair of them and leave them to themselves. . . . Even about the faults of my servants or other inferiors, if three or four times warning do no good on them, I am much tempted to despair of them, and turn them away. . . . (p. 132)

The fundamental doctrines of Christianity have come to

mean far more to him than contentious points of interpretation.

> The Creed, the Lord's Prayer and the Ten Commandments do find me now the most acceptable and plentiful matter for all my meditations. They are to me as my daily bread and drink. And as I can speak or write of them over and over again, so I had rather read or hear of them than of any of the school niceties which once so much pleased me. (p. 107)

But Baxter does not allow himself to be complacent about this change either; he suspects a certain decay in his mental energy, and an aversion from attempting difficult things. On the whole, however, he concludes that the alteration is for the better. He does not take any piece of true learning to be useless, but 'That is the best doctrine and study which maketh men better and tendeth to make them happy.' (p. 109)

Experience has taught him the 'greatness and excellence of love and praise', whereas in his youth he placed a high value on grieving for sins, and was continually poring over his own shortcomings. Now self-examination is subordinated to the higher work of meditation on God and heavenly blessedness: 'For I perceive that it is the object that altereth and elevateth the mind . . . and that the love of the end is it that is the poise or spring which setteth every wheel a-going . . .' (p. 113)

Baxter in maturity is more conscious of his ignorance and more modest about his intellectual capacity than in his youth, though he cannot help being aware that his mind is actually better furnished than it was then. Now, however, he values good men above learned ones, for he perceives that 'we are all yet in the dark'. His judgement of men in general is more balanced than of old; the bad are not so bad nor the good so faultless as once he thought, and he has learnt to be far more suspicious of the professedly pious. The praise and blame of others mean much less to him than they did, though he does not attribute this simply to an increase in humility, but also to a glut of human applause. A retired and impoverished life does not grieve him: 'I have nothing in this world which I could not easily let go; but to get satisfying apprehensions of the other world is the great and grievous difficulty.' (p. 124)

Baxter's breadth of sympathy, so different from the intolerance of his youth, comes out in his treatment of those whose forms of religious belief differ from his own. The plight of the heathen distresses him, and he is inclined now to extend his charity to all lovers of God; but this does not prevent him from being more deeply afflicted than ever by the disagreements between Christians. 'Except the case of the infidel world, nothing is so sad and grievous to my thoughts as the case of the divided churches.' (p. 118)

The life-review ends on a penitential note. Baxter has not forgotten that this self-analysis, intended for the perusal of his fellow-Christians, is in some sense a confession before God and an unburdening of his own conscience, so that its conclusion is a prayer.

In the summary of Baxter's motives for undertaking his autobiography, first place is given to his desire to render praise to God: 'As travellers and seamen use to do after great adventures and deliverances, I hereby satisfy my conscience, in praising the blessed Author of all those undeserved mercies which have filled up my life . . .' (p. 129) But although there are occasional ejaculatory prayers that remind us of this underlying purpose, the habitual slant of the book is not Godwards but towards the reader, who is sometimes directly addressed. The *Autobiography* is a vindication, an explanation, a warning, an encouragement. It is not devotional or speculative in tone, but on the whole expository, and Baxter is conscious of his duty as historian as well as teacher.

He expressly says that he has learned from experience to be

sceptical about the honesty of historians, who from partiality, if not from deliberate malice, will distort facts and falsify evidence. Living in an epoch of violent political and religious upheavals, he has been disgusted by 'The prodigious lies that have been published in this age in matters of fact, with unblushing confidence, even where thousands or multitudes of eye- and ear-witnesses knew all to be false. . . .' (p. 126) In treating of contemporary affairs, he himself has never gone wilfully against the truth; but, because he knows how liable the human mind is to bias and error, he warns his readers that he expects no unthinking assent from them, but is prepared to have his own accounts tested by the evidence of other reliable witnesses. Moreover, to escape the charge of partiality, he has refrained from detailed descriptions of his opponents— 'although, indeed, the true description of persons is much of the very life of history, and especially of the history of the age which I have lived in . . .'. (p. 128) Only in the case of the Cromwellians and sectaries has he relaxed this rule, for the typically Baxterian reason that nobody could suspect him to have opposed them for motives of interest.

The portraits that do occur in the *Autobiography* are so interesting that one can only regret Baxter's self-denying ordinance; but the way in which he condemns his own sharpness of invective in controversy suggests that he suspected himself of a degree of intolerance unbecoming to a historian. Because he was on his guard against his natural vehemence, the tone of his general judgements and historical summaries is eminently fair-minded. He did not conceive it to be his duty to give his readers a sustained narrative of public events; the episode of Charles and the Boscobel oak, for example, is merely alluded to as something 'sufficiently declared to the world'; but that he took his mission as a historian seriously is evident from his introduction to his account of the causes leading to the Civil War: 'It is of very great moment here to understand the quality of the persons which adhered to the king and to the parliament, with their reasons.' (p. 68) The largeness of his undertaking became, in later years, an oppression. After giving some account of the anti-popery excitement that prevailed in 1678 and 1679, Baxter remarks: 'But my unfitness, and the torrent of late matter here, stops me from proceeding to insert the history of this age. It is done, and like to be done, so copiously by others that these shreds will be of small signification.' (p. 246)

The purely historical value of Baxter's narrative of his life and times is beyond question very great, but how he compares as a chronicler with Burnet and Clarendon is a question that does not come within the scope of this study. It is not primarily as a writer of memoirs but as a scrutiniser of his own personal development that Baxter claims our interest. Yet there is something self-revealing in his very treatment of public affairs, and especially of the Civil War episodes. After fifteen years, the recollection of the battle of Naseby makes him suddenly abandon the past for the present tense; or he tells of his encounter with Colonel Purefoy, one of Cromwell's confidants, with a similar vivid flash of memory:

> And as soon as I had spoken what I did of the army, magisterially he answereth me, 'Let me hear no more of that. If Nol Cromwell should hear any soldier speak but such a word, he would cleave his crown. You do them wrong; it is not so.' (p. 51)

Lack of affectation is one of the principal qualities of Baxter's style, as it was of his personality. His 'strong natural inclination to speak of every subject just as it is, and to call a spade a spade' (p. 131) stands him in excellent stead, whether he is dealing with public or private affairs. An extremely persuasive preacher, he writes, in these personal memoirs, in an easy and usually informal way. Images and illustrations are used with considerable freedom and force, but what arrests us is not so often the felicitious phrase as the mature wisdom that Baxter can pack into some comment. Speaking of pride, he says: 'It's a wonder, that it should be a *possible* sin to men that still carry about with them, in soul and body, such humbling matter of remedy as we all do.' (p. 124) Though so much of his writing had been violently polemical, he is eventually capable of reflecting that 'While we wrangle here in the dark, we are dying, and passing to the world that will decide all our controversies. And the safest passage thither is by peaceable holiness.' (p. 218) The *Autobiography* gains its great distinction less from Baxter's prose style than from the exceptionally fine quality of his mind and heart.

His personal memoirs came to an abrupt stop in January 1685. In the following month Charles II died, and within a few weeks of the accession of James II, Baxter had been arrested on the charge of attacking the bishops and secular authorities under cover of a 'scandalous and seditious book', entitled *A Paraphrase of the New Testament*. He was brought to trial at the end of May, before Judge Jeffreys, and an extremely lively eye-witness's account has survived among the papers collected by Matthew Sylvester.[1]

Baxter was by this time a man of seventy, and much worn by incessant ill-health and sporadic ill-treatment. Jeffreys, allegedly the worse for drink, bullied and browbeat Baxter's counsel, and abused Baxter himself as an old rogue, an old schismatical knave, a hypocritical villain, 'a conceited, stubborn, fanatical dog that did not conform when he might have been preferred (to a bishopric)'. Ignoring the actual issue that was before him, Jeffreys threatened to have Baxter

[1] Quoted at length by J. M. Lloyd Thomas in his edition of the *Autobiography*, Appendix A.

whipped through the streets as a ringleader of the snivelling, seditious Nonconformists. After an utter travesty of a trial, Baxter was sentenced to a heavy fine and to imprisonment until it should be paid. He would have remained in prison till his death, for he had no intention of paying the fine or petitioning for release, had not Lord Powis intervened on his behalf. His final years were, in fact, comparatively peaceful, for he lived to see the flight of James II and the establishment of the Protestant Succession.

Perhaps his dying words will serve as well as any other testimony to suggest his invincible sincerity and goodness. Towards the end, tortured by pain, he said to his friends. 'Do not think the worse of religion for what you see me suffer'. The day before he died, on being asked how he felt, he replied, 'I have pain—there is no arguing against sense; but I have peace, I have peace.'

The value of even the secular, historical pages of the *Autobiography* largely derives from the spiritual quality of Baxter's integrity. Intellectually and morally he was, without doubt, a man of exceptional calibre; but, beyond that, he was a man of prayer and a servant of God. He could survive all reverses and losses with his spirit unimpaired because, ultimately, his life was founded upon a spiritual relationship, the relation of his soul to its Master. And this was not subject to violent emotional fluctuations because it was regulated by the practice of meditation. *The Saints' Everlasting Rest* is, in the words of its subtitle, 'A Directory for the getting and keeping of the Heart in Heaven: By the diligent practice of that Excellent unknown Duty of Heavenly Meditation.' Baxter's own mastery of that art has a direct bearing upon his autobiographical work, for it involved him in prolonged and searching analysis of his own inclinations and motives. The judicious tone, so conspicuous in the *Breviate* as well as in the *Autobiography*, is characteristic of a man trained in self-knowledge and in the exercise of sincerity.

Baxter's heart was in his devotion to God, in his pastoral work, his preaching, his writing and his studies; but he lived for a while at the centre of momentous events in England, and the ways of the world were far more intelligible to him than they were to such visionaries as George Fox or John Bunyan. This outward-looking capacity, which equipped him to deal with public affairs, combines with his powers of self-judgement to give to his *Autobiography* its peculiar and impressive strength.

'A kind of picture
left behind me . . . '

Autobiography is a strange hybrid. It would be an over-simplification to regard it merely as an off-shoot of biography, which in its turn is a scion of history; yet this aspect of its origin has perhaps been neglected in our concentration upon the introspective autobiography. This came to flower in seventeenth-century England chiefly, as we have seen, because of the double pressure of humanism and puritanism, both urging upon men the extreme importance of individual responsibility. But there are autobiographers of this period who are concerned more with the outer than the inner life. It is not the process of spiritual growth that interests them so much as the pageant of events—private and domestic events, maybe, unworthy of the attention of the serious chronicle-writer, but memorable and full of significance for those who experienced them.

These factual autobiographies seem to owe their impetus to two closely connected ideas, extremely commonplace today but not taken for granted before the Renaissance. The first is that the lives of quite ordinary men and women may be worth recording; the second, that everyday happenings are not necessarily trivial.

Historians of Antiquity and of the Middle Ages had written the lives of rulers and saints, almost always showing themselves to be more concerned with the characteristics that their heroes shared with other exemplars of the same ethical type than with the peculiarities which distinguished them as individuals. Memorable deeds and words are recorded, but not those traits which enable the reader to picture the man as he lived his daily life. These historians had a sense of decorum which made it inconceivable that they should retail small particulars of appearance, gesture, manners or tastes. The purpose of classical and medieval biography was to present examples, either for imitation or warning. The Fall of Princes was a theme that never became wearisome, nor did men tire of hagiography. Only lives of heroic proportions were then considered worthy of record.

With the Renaissance, biographers began to commemorate men of learning, as well as the powerful and the pious. Sir Thomas More's version of the Latin life of Pico della Mirandola, written about 1505, is the first English biography of a man without either royal or ecclesiastical rank. For another century and a half, however, biography in England was too often confused with panegyric. It is not until the mid-seventeenth century that we find for the first time, in the *Lives* of Izaak Walton, that interest in the minute details of ordinary life which has characterised the best biography ever since his day.

Dryden contended that biography excelled other branches of history in pleasure and instruction, partly because its greater concentration produces a strong, unified impression, partly because it can treat of 'minute circumstances and trivial passages of life'.

> Here you are led into the private lodgings of the Heroe: you see him in his undress, and are made Familiar with his most private actions and conversations. . . . The Pageantry of Life is taken away; you see the poor reasonable Animal, as naked as ever nature

made him; are made acquainted with his passions and follies, and find the *Demy-God a Man*.[1]

The idea that a man's private actions may be interesting to other men may owe something to the spirit of scientific detachment which developed after the Renaissance; it certainly is connected with the growing sense of social equality. Dryden brings out clearly the anti-heroic element in it. There is a pleasure, he implies, in reducing the great to small proportions, in puncturing pretensions and establishing a bond of common human weakness between the subject of the biography and the readers. Today inquisitiveness about other people's lives has become an insatiable appetite; and though we may deplore the more outrageous manifestations of it in the press and on the screen, we all to some degree share the curiosity and regard it as perfectly natural. Before the Restoration, however, it very rarely found literary expression.

The stirrings of democratic and egalitarian sentiment in England during the sixteenth and seventeenth centuries gave an impetus to chroniclers of ordinary lives, whether their own or other men's; and there was another notion gradually insinuating itself into the common mind—the notion that a man's quotidian life is more real, more interesting, more important, than the inner life of the spirit. If earthly existence is conceived to be a momentous interlude in a drama of eternal dimensions, there is no urgent need to record its dailinesses. This is not to say that such a conception cannot underlie an autobiography. That of St Augustine is, of course, based on precisely this premiss. But in an age of expanding mercantile activity and growing materialism, there is every

---

[1] *The Life of Plutarch*, prefixed to *Plutarch's Lives, translated from the Greek by Several Hands*, 1683. Reprinted as an Appendix to V. da Sola Pinto's anthology, *Introduction to English Biography in the Seventeenth Century*, 1951, p. 202.

encouragement to attach a high importance to the transactions of every day. The habit of keeping diaries developed during the Tudor period, and towards the end of the seventeenth century we get a great number of diaries and journals, most of them quite objective in tone.

The *Liber Famelicus* of Sir James Whitelock[1] will serve to exemplify the simplest type of chronicle autobiography. He began to write it on the 18th of April 1609, with the prefatory remark, 'In it I entend to set downe memorialls for my posterity of things most properly concerning myself and my familye.' Whitelock, an eminent lawyer and judge, who met a number of distinguished people during his active life, begins by outlining his ancestry; there are a few anecdotes about his brothers; he gives a brief but interesting account of his schooling under Richard Mulcaster at 'Marchantaylours', and of his studies at Oxford. The births, and too often the deaths, of his own children are recorded, together with the names of their godparents; and deaths of eminent acquaintances are noted throughout the memoir. Occasionally there is a touch of pathos, as when he described the death of his aged mother: 'She went away even withe olde age as a candle that goethe out.' Or we may smile at his lists of Christmas presents received—several does, a keg of sturgeon, a fat turkey, a fat swan, a sugar loaf— and at the comment: 'These I set down *inter famelica*, that my son may hereafter see these frendly kindnesses doon to me, which ar not so usual to those that ly in London as to those in the countrye, and that he may endeavour to live worthy of the like.' (p. 32) But on the whole this memoir is an unemotional, factual account of his career; it is written without any literary pretensions, and its interest is primarily historical.

Sir James Whitelock explicitly states his motive for compiling his *Liber Famelicus*, and as his son, Bulstrode Whitelock,

[1] Published by the Camden Society, 1857

followed in his footsteps and outdistanced him in fame, we may conclude that the book served its immediate purpose well. But sometimes we are left wondering why a man, of no great distinction, should have gone to the pains of writing his life-history. Adam Martindale, for instance, a Nonconformist minister of Lancashire yeoman stock; what determined him to write his autobiography?[1] His children were already dead; he was not an eminent man. The sententious 'Observations' sandwiched between the chapters suggest that the book was intended as a work of edification; but one of its great merits is its freedom from the unctuousness and pious cant that characterise far too many of the life-stories of seventeenth-century dissenters.

Adam Martindale, for all his Nonconformist conscience, was no Malvolio, as we can judge from his account of his father's funeral:

> Considering how good a father he had beene, and how fashion-ably he (in the time of his prosperity) had lived among his neighbours, we thought it convenient to bring him home handsomely out of his owne, and so we did. For all that came to the house to fetch his corpse thence (beggars not excepted) were entertained with good meat, piping hot, and strong ale in great plentie ...

Moreover, after the funeral ceremony,

> There was a rich dinner readie prepared at a tavern for the kindred, and so many more as a great roome would receive, with plentie of wine and strong drinke, and for all the rest tag and rag sufficient store of such provisions as are usuall at ordinary burialls.

[1] *Life* of Adam Martindale, printed from MS. in British Museum for the Chetham Society (Remains Historical and Literary connected with the Palatine Counties of Lancaster and Chester), ed. Rev. Richard Parkinson, B.D., 1845.

A comment very typical of the thrifty author follows:

> Yet all this came to noe great matter, being discreetly ordered by
> such as were employed about it. So that I am verily persuaded
> that some funeralls have cost twice so much, that have not been
> so creditable to the cost-makers. (p. 120)

From the life-story a clear picture of the man emerges. He
was gifted with real enthusiasm for learning and teaching. A
village schoolmaster in his youth, he took up the study of
mathematics after the Act of Uniformity had deprived him of
the ministry to which he had been ordained by a Presbyterian
classis. He taught, and invented a dialling instrument, and
educated his son who was debarred from a place in either
university because of his father's political and religious in-
transigeance. Though unable to preach or officiate in public,
he became domestic chaplain to Lord and Lady Delamer. The
latter part of the book is full of his domestic trials, the deaths of
his children and his own frustrations. As a parish minister he
had been evidently extremely conscientious, preaching and
catechising in a manner that Baxter himself would have
approved.

What makes the book particularly attractive is Martindale's
strong affection for his family, especially for his parents and
his sister Jane. The narrative about Jane's escapades in London
is a most lively piece of writing. This episode happened during
his boyhood, but his manner of telling it suggests that it was a
story often repeated in the family circle.

Jane, though she lacked for nothing at home, made up her
mind to leave the pure air of her native Lancashire village for
the notoriously unhealthy London, where she had no friends.
In vain the family tried to dissuade her.

> She measured not a competencie by the same mete-wand that
> they did. Freeholders' daughters were then confined to their

felts, petticoates and wastcoates, coarse handkerchiefs about their neckes, and white cross-clothes upon their heads, with coifes under them wrought with black silk or worsted. 'Tis true the finest sort of them wore gold or silver lace upon their wastcoates, good silk laces (and store of them) about their pettiecoates, and bone laces or workes about their linnens. But the proudest of them (below the gentry) durst not have offered to weare an hood, or a scarfe, (which now every beggar's brat that can get them thinks not above her), noe, not so much as a gowne till her wedding day. And if any of them had transgressed these bounds, she would have been accounted an ambitious foole. (p. 6)

But Jane, 'having her father's spirit and her mother's beautie, no persuasions would serve, but up she would go to serve a ladie as she hoped to do, being ingenious at her needle'.

Unfortunately she gets the plague, just as they prophesied, and she is too proud to ask for money when she gets into straits. She does bring herself to ask for a goose-pie, 'to make merrie with her friends; and a lustie one was immediately sent her, cased in twig work . . .'. (p.8) But her money grew so short that 'she had thoughts to sell her haire, which was very lovely both for length and colour'. Perhaps in desperation, she marries; he is her social superior, but something of a ne'er-do-well, and they keep an inn. Eventually she returns to Lancashire, but soon sickens of smallpox and dies, very much disfigured. 'Whereas my mother,' observes Adam Martindale, 'who, notwithstanding her beautie, was very humble, lay with a cleare and seemingly smiling countenance after she was dead, as if she had beene still alive.' (p. 18)

It cannot be claimed that the whole of this autobiography is as lively as the pages about Jane, though as a document for social historians it is of exceptional value. Martindale has a high regard for factual accuracy, and a shrewd eye for detail. Moreover, the whole book is pervaded by the good sense of its author, who refused to be embittered by adversity. Though he never attempts to analyse or even to depict himself, there are plenty of revealing human touches which make the book a notable autobiography of a quite unpretentious kind.

It seems reasonable to suppose that the main impulse that moved Martindale to write his own history was the realisation that he lived in insecure and rapidly changing times. He was born in the year that Shakespeare died, and the sixty-two years of his life spanned the Civil War, the Protectorate, the Restoration and its aftermath. His own career had been thoroughly upset by the march of public events. Like other Puritans towards the end of the century, he had cause to reflect on change and decay; not merely in his own fortunes, but in the general state of the realm. A sense of insecurity often provokes the writing of small-scale history. The vast amount of *reportage* during the last war is proof of this. When everything familiar is threatened, and accustomed ways of life are liable to be transformed out of recognition, people of observant habit take up their pens. They might not have written at all, unprovoked; but they are impelled by the desire to preserve the memory of what is passing, of what may soon be past.

The Civil War was particularly provocative of memoirs. Apart from its disruptive effects, it inevitably produced people of both parties anxious to justify their own doings and to ventilate their grievances and sufferings. A few memorialists, like Clarendon and Burnet, had a real grasp of the historical importance of the great events in which their lives were involved. Most of them could see no further than their own individual horizons. They could remember adventurous days, weeks of suspense; they had suffered bereavements, reversals of fortune, financial losses, disappointments. The small doings of their private lives were magnified by their association with national catastrophes or triumphs.

These memoirs often took the form of biographies. Two of

the best are by women. Mrs Hutchinson's life of her husband is justly famous; Lady Fanshawe's story of 'Dick of Devonshire' is not as well known as it deserves to be. In so far as their own lives were identified with their husbands', the narratives have autobiographical interest too, but this is only indirect and incidental. There is, however, a remarkably interesting and very little known autobiography by a woman of strong Royalist sympathies, Lady Halkett. This is a thoroughly feminine document. It is neither reflective nor speculative; it is concerned with persons and actions, not with ideas. Though as a girl Anne Murray was drawn into a great deal of political activity, her comments on public events and eminent men are coloured far more by her passionate devotion to the Stuarts than by any historical acumen. Her life-story is recounted so vividly as to remind us that the best story-tellers are not those introspective autobiographers who are perpetually interrupting their narratives in order to ponder and probe. The best are the people who relish life for the sake of its variousness and unpredictability; those who delight in recalling and re-living the adventures and misadventures of their past. The autobiography of Anne, Lady Halkett, contains sufficient material for a full-length novel packed from cover to cover with romance, excitement and suspense. It is a retrospective narrative, written when she was an elderly woman, and the story is handled with almost a novelist's skill.

Her anonymous biographer[1] writing two years after her death, remarks that she was in the habit of keeping memoirs or diaries, 'when in the most serious manner between God and her own Soul, she was reviewing the several Periods of her Life, observing and recording, what ever might be of after-use, to preserve in her Thankfulness and Humility, or to confirm

[1] *The Life of the Lady Halkett*, Edinburgh, 1701, was prefixed to some of her Meditations, and signed S.C.

her Hope and Trust in God . . .'. But the *Autobiography* itself[1]
is strikingly free from introspection. Lady Halkett surveys her
life as a whole, and selects for extended treatment the episodes
that are fullest of dramatic and human interest. At appropriate
moments she introduces dialogue; and though invention
probably plays a larger part than memory in the construction
of these conversations, they are exceptionally lively, and add
a great deal to the verisimilitude of the story. With real
subtlety she keeps us guessing at a mystery that for years
beset her life with perplexity: was her suitor, Colonel Bamfield,
telling the truth when he affirmed, against persistent rumour,
that his wife was dead? By reserving the disclosure until the
moment in her life-history when it actually occurred, she
re-creates for herself and her readers the very atmosphere of
uncertainty in which so many years of her life were passed.
Only someone with considerable narrative skill and a strongly
developed sense of dramatic effectiveness would have refrained
from giving the secret away at the start.

The build-up of suspense is the more remarkable since
Bamfield had been discredited long before she began to write
her life-history. Dismissed from Royalist service in 1654 for
suspected double-dealing, he worked in Paris and Frankfort as
an agent of Cromwell. Returning to England at the Restoration, he was imprisoned for a year in the Tower. Not a word
about his disgrace appears in Anne Halkett's autobiography.
He wrote his own *Apologie* when living in exile in Holland, and
it was published at the Hague in 1685. From this and from his
letters it is clear that he was, as Clarendon described him, 'a wit
and man of parts'; but State papers afford plenty of evidence
that he was a plausible and unprincipled political intriguer. It

---

[1] Published by the Camden Society, 1875, edited by J. G. Nichols, who
did not complete the task, which was carried out pretty perfunctorily by
S. R. Gardiner.

can scarcely be doubted that the story of his wife's death was fabricated in order to win Anne Murray's complete allegiance. With her resourceful courage and immense integrity she was an excellent ally and accomplice. No doubt he argued that if she considered herself engaged to him, her loyalty to the Stuart cause would be doubly strong. Whatever his real feelings were for her, Bamfield certainly succeeded in persuading Anne that he truly loved her and that he was a man of honour. Her love for him was so great that it did not permit her to reproach him even when his unreliability had become a matter of common knowledge.

The *Autobiography* seems to have been written about 1678, when Lady Halkett was fifty-six. She had been a widow for eight years, and her one surviving son, Robert, had finished his studies at St Andrew's. What particularly impelled her to write the story of her life in a connected form we do not know. She was a distinguished woman, well connected, well endowed with brains and character, and she had been caught up in Royalist intrigues for many years. She was also a woman who enjoyed writing. Some of the devotional meditations printed after her death had been written before her marriage, and during her long widowhood she wrote many more, so that more than twenty titles of works in manuscript were listed by her biographer. But in her autobiography no confessional or didactic motive is apparent, nor is it the work of someone with a well-developed sense of history. She was involved in public events, she met eminent people; but her comments on the times in which she lived are not very many or very penetrating. No, it seems to have been the uniqueness of her own life that delighted her. What hopes and fears, what trials, what adventures had come her way! Prepared to re-live in imagination the excitements of bygone days, she set about her task of story-telling; and though her book is uneven and incomplete, the best passages in it show an unusual power of recollection, selection and reconstruction.

The kind of episode that she stored up in her memory or recorded in her journals was just the sort of thing that lingers in the mind of the average woman. Encounters with lovers and suitors, personal griefs and illnesses, conversations in which she scored successes, details of costume and gesture and manner—these are what seemed important to Anne Halkett when she came to write her life-story.

Her first serious love-affair, for instance, lived so vividly in her memory that even after thirty-five years she could reconstruct it with real emotional warmth and many telling details. Her mother had forbidden her to encourage the eighteen-year-old Thomas Howard, who was supposed to make a rich match; but he threatened to turn Capuchin if Anne would not have him.

> Hee grew so ill and discontented that all the howse took notice, and I did yield so farre to comply with his desire as to give him liberty one day when I was walking in ye gallery to come there and speake to me. What he saide was handsome and short, butt much disordered, for he looked pale as death, and his hand trembled when he tooke mine to leade mee, and with a great sigh said 'If I loved you lesse I could say more.' (*Autobiography*, p. 4)

Fearing that her refusal really would drive him into a monastery, Anne promised that she would never marry until she saw him first married. This concession only inflamed his ardour. He proposed a private marriage, for fear of their parents' displeasure. Anne refused to consider this, but it came to the ears of her mother, who threatened to have nothing more to do with her if she persisted in seeing the young man. They meet once more in desperation. Young Howard accuses himself:

'To thinke that I should bee ye occasion of trouble to the person
in ye earth that I love most is unsuportable': and with that he
fell downe in a chaire that was behind him, but as one without
all sense, wch I must confesse did soe much move mee, yt laing
aside all former distance I had kept him att, I sat downe upon his
knee, and laying my head neare his I suffred him to kisse me, wch
was a liberty I never gave him before, nor had nott then had I nott
seene him so overcome with griefe. (p. 8)

Though she thinks he has left the neighbourhood, he still
lingers and sends entreaties that Anne will see him once again.

In the midst of this dispute with myself what I should doe, my
hand being still upon my eyes, itt presently came in my mind
that if I blindfolded my eyes that would secure mee from seeing
him, and so I did not transgrese against my mother, and hee might
that way satisfy himselfe by speaking to mee. (p. 12)

So they met for a last farewell, but Anne did not escape her
mother's displeasure. For fourteen months she refused her
blessing, and even said once with much bitterness that she
hated the sight of her daughter. Anne was so hurt at this that
she sought advice about entering a Protestant nunnery in
Holland, but Sir Patrick Drummond, to whom her enquiries
were addressed, remonstrated with Mrs Murray, who ever
after that time treated Anne more like a friend than a child.

Presently Mr Howard returns from France, again in quest
of a rich wife. The episode that follows is extraordinarily like
the one in *Sense and Sensibility* when Marianne discovers the
fickleness of Willoughby; but Anne Murray unites with the
sensibility of Marianne a liberal portion of the good sense of
Elinor. When Howard makes no attempt to see her, Anne has
misgivings, thinking that

hee had laid all thoughts of mee aside, and was come with a
resolution to comply with his father's desire. The last opinion I
was a little confirmed in, having never received any word or

letter from him in ten days after his return, and meeting him
accidentally where I was walking he crossed the way, and another
time was in the roome when I came in to visitt some young
ladys, and neither of these times tooke any notice of mee more
then of one I have never seene. I confese I was a little disordered
att itt, butt made noe conclusions till I saw what time would
produce. (p. 17)

Howard eventually does send excuses, saying that he is
purposely dissembling, and is visiting a number of young ladies
in order to shake off suspicion; but an Earl's daughter beguiles
him, and they are reported to be in love; at which some smiled,
and said it might be with her wit but certainly not with her
beauty, 'for,' says Anne with delightful candour, 'she had as
little of that as my selfe.' But the rumours are true. He secretly
marries the Lady Elizabeth Mordaunt. Anne is outraged, but
like Elinor Dashwood she keeps her self-possession:

> I was alone in my sister's chamber when I read the letter, and
> flinging my selfe downe on her bed, I said 'Is this the man for
> whom I have suffred so much? Since hee hath made him selfe
> unworthy my love, hee is unworthy my anger or concerne;'
> and rising immediately, I wentt outt into the next roome to my
> super, as unconcernedly as if I had never had an interest in him,
> nor had never lost itt . . . (p. 18)

After this display of spirit, it is a little sad to read that 'Nothing
troubled me more than my mother's laughing att mee.'

But Thomas Howard was not the man who truly captured
her heart; nor was Sir James Halkett, the good and considerate
man whom she eventually married. The love of her life was
Joseph Bamfield, who, as a Royalist colonel, enters the story
when Anne is about twenty-five. Her brother Will made them
acquainted, and Anne soon got caught up in the Royalist
intrigues in which both Bamfield and Will Murray were
already deeply implicated.

From babyhood she had been quite closely associated with the royal household. Her father had been tutor to Prince Charles, later Charles I, and had been made Provost of Eton in recognition of this. After his death, which occurred when Anne was a very small child, his widow was made governess to the Duke of Gloucester and the Princess Elizabeth. It was therefore not at all surprising that Anne willingly aided Bamfield in the plot, in which he was the prime mover, to smuggle the Duke of York out of England in the spring of 1648. It was her part to provide the disguise.

Having obtained the boy's measurements,

> When I gave the measure to my tailor to enquire how much mohaire would serve to make a petticoate and wastcoate to a young gentlewoman of that bignese and stature, hee considered itt a long time, and said hee had made many gownes and suites, butt hee had never made any to such a person in his life. I thought he was in the right; but his meaning was, hee had never seene any woman of so low a stature have so big a wast; however, hee made itt as exactly fitt as if hee had taken the measure himself. Itt was a mixed mohaire of a light haire couler and blacke, and ye under-petticoate was scarlett. (p. 21)

Touches like this, trifles accurately remembered, often occur in Anne Halkett's autobiography. They not only give solidity to what she is describing, but they also give us a glimpse of her own practical and womanly scale of values. The climax of the exciting story of the Duke of York's escape is enlivened by *minutiae* of the same kind. Anne and her maid Miriam are waiting apprehensively for the arrival by water of Colonel Bamfield and the young prince; they are in a private house by the Thames-side. Soon after ten at night

> I heard a great noise of many as I thought coming up staires, wch I expected to be soldiers to take mee, but it was a pleasing dis-appointment, for ye first that came in was ye Duke, who with

much joy I took in my armes and gave God thanks. His Highnese called 'Quickely quickely dress me' and putting of his cloaths I dressed him in the wemen's habitt that was prepared, which fitted his Highnese very well, and was very pretty in it. After he had eaten something I made ready while I was idle lest his Highnese should be hungry, and having sent for a Woodstreet-cake (wch I knew he loved) to take in the barge . . . (p. 22)

the prince leaves with Bamfield, and in spite of contrary winds they reach Gravesend, where a ship is waiting to convey him to Holland.

Not long after this, Colonel Bamfield proposed marriage to Anne. His wife, from whom he had been living apart because of her Parliamentary connections, has recently died; or so he said, and so he made Anne believe. After refusing him more than once, she consents, promising to marry him as soon as political conditions make it convenient. Her comment on this decision is characteristically honest, generous and dignified:

I know I may bee condemned as one that was too easily prevailed with, but this I must desire to be considered, hee was one who I had beene conversantt with for severall yeares before: one that professed a great friendship to my beloved brother Will; hee was unquestionably loyall, handsome, a good schollar, wch gave him the advantages of writing and speaking well, and the cheefest ornamentt hee had was a devout life and conversation. Att least hee made itt appeare such to mee, and whatever misfortune hee brought upon mee I will doe him that right as to acknowledge I learnt from him many excellent lessons of piety and vertue, and to abhorre and detest all manner of vice. (p. 26)

For the next five years Anne considers herself engaged to him, though rumours persist that Mrs Bamfield is still alive. Finally Sir James Halkett brings her incontrovertible proof that she is indeed living; but even then Anne has not seen the last of Bamfield. He comes uninvited to her lodging in London, to ask whether she is already married to Sir James.

I asked why hee inquired. He said because if I was nott, hee would then propose something that hee thought might bee both for his advantage and mine: but if I were, hee would wish mee joy, butt never trouble mee more. I said nothing for a while, for I hated lying, and I saw there might bee some inconvenience to tell the truth, and (Lord pardon the equivocation!) I sayd *I am* outt aloud, and secretly said *nott*. Hee immediately rose up and said 'I wish you and him much hapinese together' and, taking his leave, from that time to this I never saw him nor heard from him. (p. 99)

There is poetic justice in this turning of the tables upon a persistent equivocator, and it recalls the rather similar stratagem by which Anne as a girl managed to keep the letter of her promise to her mother by going blindfold to meet young Thomas Howard.

From her biographer we learn that Lady Halkett died at the age of seventy-seven widely esteemed and beloved for her piety, talents and learning; and nobody reading her own account of her life could doubt that she was a woman to inspire both love and respect. Men and women alike could rely on her for unswerving friendship; her servants, clearly, were devoted to her; to strangers in need she was charitable to a heroic degree. In later life she won a considerable reputation for her knowledge of physic and her skill in doctoring the sick. In the autobiography there is an interesting account of how, after the Battle of Dunbar, she treated at least sixty wounded soldiers at her lodging in Kinross. Clearly she was a born nurse. She heartened the downcast, gave extra dressings to those who were capable of looking after themselves, and with the help of her maid and a manservant tackled even the lousiest and most noisome cases.

One particularly was in that degree who was shott through the arm that none was able to stay in the roome, but all left mee. Accidentally a gentleman came in, who seeing mee (not without reluctancy) cutting off the man's sleeve of his doublet, wch was hardly fitt to be toutched, hee was so charitable as to take a knife and cutt it off and fling in ye fire. (p. 63)

The same gentleman, incidentally, reported her good deeds to the King and Council. Not only was Anne commended, and later rewarded, but surgeons and temporary hospitals were organised in various Scottish towns as a result of her pioneer work for the wounded.

Besides being strong in charity and fortitude, she had plenty of high-spirited courage too. No episode in the book illustrates this better than her treatment of a band of Cromwellian soldiers who were making themselves a nuisance to the Dunfermline household at Fyvie. Lady Dunfermline, who was pregnant at the time, begged Anne to intercede with her countrymen, but at the same time warned her of the risk she ran in confronting them. Anne at once went down with her maid, and addressed herself to the self-styled 'major' in charge of the troop.

As soone as I came amongst them, the first question they asked mee was if I were the English whore that came to meet the King, and all set their pistolls just against me. (I had armed myself before by seeking assistance from Him who only could protect me from their fury, and I did so much rely upon itt that I had not the least feare, tho naturally I am the greatest coward living.) I told them I owned myselfe to bee an English woman, and to honor the King, butt for the name they gave mee I abhorred itt; butt my coming to them was nott to dispute for my selfe, butt to tell them I was sorry to heare that any of the English nation, who was generally esteemed the most civill people of the world, should give so much occasion to be thought barbarously rude, as they had done since their comming into that howse, where they found none to resist them, but by the contrary whatever they called for, either to themselves or their horses, was ordered by my Lady to be given them.

With her customary sense of the value of direct speech as an aid to narrative, Anne now resorts to it:

'What advantage (said I) can you propose to yourselves to fright a person of honour who is great with child, and few butt children and weemen in the howse? and if by your disorder any misfortune happen to my Lady, or any belonging to the familly, you may expect to be called to account for itt, because I am very confidentt you have no allowance from your officers to be uncivill to any, and I am sure it is more to your interest to obleege all you can then to disobleege them, for the one will make you loved, the other hated; and judge which will be the most for your advantage.'

This blend of firmness and persuasion had an excellent effect. The soldiers heard her out, flung their pistols on the table, and promised that they would not molest the meanest in the family, so long as they were provided with meat and drink and other necessaries. 'And they did so keepe theyre word that my Lady Dunfermline was by theyre staying in the howse secured from many insolencys that were practised in other places.' (p. 68)

Lady Halkett's *Autobiography* is an exceptionally straightforward narrative, unmarred by any attempt to frame a cautionary or exemplary tale. Such pious reflections as occur come into the story naturally, and are patently sincere. She admits to indiscretions and errors of judgement, but on the whole she feels that she has not comported herself badly in a life full of trials and tensions; and her readers can hardly fail to agree with this underlying, though unspoken, conviction. Though the greatest merit of the book is its unaffected handling of a personal, private life-story, it does also open a window on the troubled years when the Royalists were plotting the restoration of the monarchy. Secret meetings, escapes from prison, letters in cypher, disguises, these were part of the very stuff of the life of Lady Halkett before her marriage. Looking back on those troubled years, she chronicled them with a real appreciation of their romance.

Although a good deal of material from her autobiography was utilised by the biographer who wrote a prefatory memoir to the *Meditations* published in 1701, two years after her death, the record itself was not written with any idea of publication. Very few English memoirs were printed before 1660, and many of the post-Restoration lives and diaries known to us today were first made public in the nineteenth century. However, a vogue for memoirs, fictitious as well as true, crossed the Channel with Charles II and his court, and many translations of French memoirs were made during the last quarter of the seventeenth century. Gilbert Burnet, the distinguished historian of the Civil War, writing in 1673 remarks:

> Every year we get new *Memoires* of some one Great Person or another. And though there are great Indiscretions committed, in publishing many Secrets and Papers, not fit for Publick View: yet this way of Writing takes now more in the World than any sort of History ever did.[1]

A generation later, John Sheffield, Earl of Mulgrave and Duke of Buckingham, opened his own rather brief and disappointing memoirs with an interesting comment on the popularity of this mode of writing:

> Having observed that Memoirs and accounts of persons tho' not very considerable, when written by themselves, have been greedily read, and often found useful; not only for knowledge of things past, but as cautions for the future: I have chosen to imploy some part of that leisure (which I have had by intervals, and which by reason of decaying health and vigour I know not how

[1] *Memoirs of the Lives and Action of James & William, Dukes of Hamilton & Castleherald,* 1677, Preface.

to spend better) in setting down exactly and impartially all I
could remember of myself, fit to be made publick; a kind of
picture left behind me to my friends and family, very like, tho'
neither well painted, nor handsome.[1]

What is the secret of the fascination of these autobiographies
of 'persons not very considerable'? Surely not their usefulness;
even though, as Buckingham alleges, they may enrich our
knowledge of the past or, conceivably, serve as useful warnings.
That adverb of his, 'greedily', suggests that they satisfy a
craving; but why did those eighteenth-century readers relish
so keenly the memoirs of their contemporaries? And why does
the vast semi-literate public of today devour personal gossip
with such an insatiable appetite? Inquisitiveness about one's
neighbours is as primitive a trait as the desire to talk about one's
own exploits; but social and literary conventions have at some
periods inhibited, and at others encouraged, these foibles.
Why other people's private lives should be of such inexhaustible
interest to the citizens of modern pluto-democracies is a
question perhaps better tackled by the sociologist than by the
literary historian. He, however, can safely assert that in England
the appetite for memoirs first became noticeable in the seventeenth century. The very word Biography did not become
current before the sixteen-eighties. Nor was the autobiography
a recognised literary *genre* much before the Restoration. In
the course of this book, various causes have been suggested to
account for this phenomenon, and they may now be briefly
recapitulated.

The autobiographical impulse is, of course, latent in every
age, for it is closely allied to the basic need for expressing
personal tensions that also generates poetry and fictitious
narrative. But it received a great stimulus in western Europe
as a result of the Renaissance. The focus of men's interests

[1] *Works*, 1723, vol. II, p. 3.

shifted from eternity to time, and from the community to the individual. As the spirit of scientific enquiry grew stronger, the old exhortation *Nosce Teipsum* became a new challenge. Add to this the gradual shift of emphasis, in England, from the aristocratic to the democratic ideal, and it will be seen how many factors favoured the development of autobiography at this particular period. The Civil War gave an impetus to the writing of factual memoirs; the growth of protestant sectarianism produced a large crop of conversion-narratives.

Most of the people who attempted to write their own lives at this time were not literary artists; they did not address themselves to a wide public. The more aristocratic writers of memoirs usually intended them simply for their immediate families; the Puritans had in mind their own congregations. Nevertheless, what they wrote has an interest more far-reaching than they dreamed of. Even minor memoirs of a bygone age are apt to be rewarding, for there is a peculiar pleasure in being admitted to the confidence of men and women whose lives were so differently ordered from our own. We step into a society based on very different assumptions from ours, yet we are conscious of a close, human kinship with these our predecessors. The dramatist and novelist may be able to create characters that work more subtly upon the imagination than do these creatures of flesh and blood; yet there they stand, solid witnesses to actual experience, and there is no gainsaying them.

To deal adequately with the very numerous autobiographies written in England between 1660 and the end of the century would be a life's work for a scholar, and one to attract the social historian rather than the student of literature. This brief study aims only at indicating the various types of life-story that are to be found among the annals of this period.

'The true object of autobiography', says Georg Misch,

'is the revelation of the full content of the life of an individual considered as a characteristic whole, whether that revelation is developed purely from within as the story of a soul, or condensed into a portrayal of character, or given palpable shape as a record of the outward activity of the inner life.'[1] How clearly, it may be asked, was this object perceived by the people whose autobiographies we have been considering? Bunyan, though he set down the poignant story of a soul, certainly did not propose to himself the revelation of the full content of his life; nor did Browne, though he achieved a subtle portrayal of character. The *Lives* of Herbert and of Lady Halkett are incomplete, but both writers had a strong sense of themselves as actors participating in the exciting drama of life. Baxter had the ability to counterpoint the analysis of his spiritual development with a critical account of contemporary history; yet his literary remains, as he left them, were so cumbrous as to be unreadable. Not one of them fulfils all the conditions. Yet all manage to convey across the centuries the authenticity, the uniqueness, of their experience. By each our knowledge of human nature is extended and enriched.

And here, after all, is the ultimate and very simple justification for the reading of biography, and fiction, and even gossip-columns and the *News of the World*. Human nature is so infinitely diversified, so inexhaustibly odd, that we feel a need to widen the boundaries of our own personal experience of people. We may want to compensate ourselves for the restrictions of daily life, or to assure ourselves of our own normality, or to reinforce complacency by laughing at the spectacle of other men's frailties and follies. No matter how many friends and acquaintances we may possess, no matter how far we may have travelled, we still need to supplement what we have learned at first hand. As we grow older, we tend to turn to the records

[1] *A History of Autobiography in Antiquity*, 1950, p. 65.

of lives actually lived rather than to novels. And if biographies afford us these satisfactions, how much more vividly do autobiographies of honest merit remind us that truth genuinely is stranger than fiction, and more valid too. As we read them, we lose and find ourselves; we are enlightened, entertained, and liberated from the too narrow confines of time, place and circumstance.

Selected Bibliography

GENERAL

MISCH, GEORG. *A History of Autobiography in Antiquity.* Trans. E. W. Dickes. Routledge & Kegan Paul, 1950.

BURR, A. R. *The Autobiography: a critical and comparative study.* Constable, 1909.

BATES, E. STUART. *Inside Out: An Introduction to Autobiography.* Oxford, 1936.

STAUFFER, D. A. *English Biography before 1700.* Harvard, 1930.

PINTO, V. DA S. *Introduction to English Biography in the seventeenth century.* Harrap, 1951.

MAJOR, J. C. *The Role of Personal Memoirs in English Biography.* Philadelphia, 1935.

SMITH, D. NICHOL. *Characters from the Histories and Memoirs of the seventeenth century.* Oxford, 1918.

GRIERSON, H. J. C. *Cross-currents in English Literature of the seventeenth century.* Chatto & Windus, 1929.

WILLEY, B. *The Seventeenth-Century Background.* Chatto & Windus, 1934.

BUSH, D. *English Literature in the earlier seventeenth century.* Clarendon Press, 1945.

CHAPTER III: *Sir Thomas Browne*

DUNN, W. P. *Sir Thomas Browne: a study in religious philosophy.* Minneapolis, 1950.

GOSSE, E. *Sir Thomas Browne.* (English Men of Letters.) Macmillan, 1905.

LEROY, O. *Le Chevalier Thomas Browne*. Paris, 1931.

MERTON, E. S. *Science and Imagination in Sir Thomas Browne*. New York, 1949.

PETERSSON, R. T. *Sir Kenelm Digby*. Cape, 1956.

DOWDEN, E. *Puritan and Anglican*. Kegan Paul, 1900.

MORE, P. E. *Shelburne Essays*, 6th Series. Putnam, 1909.

PATER, W. *Appreciations*. Macmillan, 1899.

RAVEN, C. E. *English Naturalists*. Cambridge, 1947.

SAINTSBURY, G. Chapter in *Cambridge History of Eng. Lit.*, 1911.

STEPHEN, L. *Hours in a Library*, 2nd Series. Smith, Elder, 1876.

STRACHEY, L. *Books and Characters*. Chatto & Windus, 1922.

WHIBLEY, C. *Essays in Biography*. Constable, 1913.

CHAPTER IV: *Lord Herbert of Cherbury*

LEE, S. Introduction and notes to 2nd (revised) edition of *The Autobiography*. Routledge, 1906.

HERFORD, C. H. Introduction to Gregynog Press edition, 1928.

HUTCHESON, H. E. Introduction to *De Religione Laici*. Yale, 1944.

MOORE SMITH, G. C. Introduction to the *Poems*. Oxford, 1923.

BUSH, D. *English Literature in the earlier seventeenth century* (Clarendon Press, 1945) discusses Herbert as Poet (pp. 151–3); Autobiographer (pp. 227–8); Philosopher (pp. 332–3).

WILLEY, B. *The Seventeenth-Century Background* (Chatto & Windus, 1934) has a section on Herbert as a philosopher, pp. 121–133.

WILLEY, B. 'Lord Herbert of Cherbury, a Spiritual Quixote of the seventeenth century.' *Essays and Studies of the English Association*, xxvii, 1941.

BLUNDEN, E. *Votive Tablets*. Cobden-Sanderson, 1931. 'The Knight's Story.'

CHAPTER V : *John Bunyan*

BROWN, JOHN. *John Bunyan*. (Tercentenary Edition.) Hulbert Publishing Co., 1928.

FROUDE, H. *John Bunyan*. (English Men of Letters.) Macmillan, 1880.

HALE WHITE, W. *Bunyan*. Hodder & Stoughton, 1905.

HARRISON, G. B. *John Bunyan, A Study in Personality*. Dent, 1928.

LINDSAY, J. *John Bunyan, Maker of Myths*. Methuen, 1937.

SHARROCK, R. *John Bunyan*. Hutchinson, 1954.

TALON, H. *John Bunyan, the Man and his Works*. Rockcliff, 1951.

TINDALL, W. Y. *John Bunyan, Mechanick Preacher*. Columbia, 1934.

BARCLAY, R. *The Inner Life of the Religious Societies of the Commonwealth*. 1876.

DOWDEN, E. *Puritan and Anglican*. Kegan Paul, 1900.

HALLER, W. *The Rise of Puritanism*. Columbia, 1938.

JAMES, W. *Varieties of Religious Experience*. Longmans, Green, 1902.

MORE, P. E. *Shelburne Essays*, 6th Series. Putnam, 1900.

PRATT, J. B. *The Religious Consciousness*. New York, 1921.

TULLOCH, J. *English Puritanism and its Leaders*. Edinburgh, 1861.

WHITING, C. E. *Studies in English Puritanism, 1660–1688*. S.P.C.K., 1931.

WHITLEY, W. T. *A History of British Baptists*. Kingsgate Press, 1932.

CHAPTER VI : *Richard Baxter*

POWICKE, F. O. *A Life of the Revd. Richard Baxter, 1651–1691*. Cape, 1924.

POWICKE, F. O. *The Revd. Richard Baxter: Under the Cross, 1662–1691*. Cape, 1927.

LADELL, A. R. *Richard Baxter: Puritan and Mystic.* S.P.C.K., 1925.

MARTIN, H. *Puritanism and Richard Baxter.* S.C.M. Press, 1954.

MORGAN, I. *The Nonconformity of Richard Baxter.* Epworth Press, 1946.

COLERIDGE, S. T. *Notes on English Divines,* ed. D. Coleridge. Moxon, 1853.

STEPHEN, SIR. J. *Essays in Ecclesiastical Biography.* Longmans, 1849.

HENSLEY HENSON, H. *Puritanism in England.* Hodder & Stoughton, 1912.

MARTZ, L. *The Poetry of Meditation.* Yale, 1955.

HALLER, W. *Liberty and Reformation in the Puritan Revolution.* Columbia, 1955.

MILLER, P. & JOHNSON, H. *The Puritans.* American Book Co., 1938.

See also the books on Puritanism mentioned in the bibliography to the chapter on Bunyan.

Index

Index

VERMONT ⚥ COLLEGE
MONTPELIER VT.

WITHDRAWN

Date D

AP 07 '90
JUN 2 '98

Demco 293-5